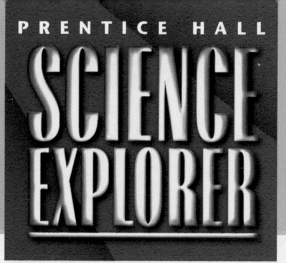

PRENTICE HALL

SCIENCE EXPLORER

Chemical
Interactions

PRENTICE HALL
Needham, Massachusetts
Upper Saddle River, New Jersey

PRENTICE HALL SCIENCE EXPLORER

Chemical Interactions

Program Resources
Student Edition
Annotated Teacher's Edition
Teaching Resources Book with Color Transparencies
Chemical Interactions Materials Kits

Program Components
Integrated Science Laboratory Manual
Integrated Science Laboratory Manual, Teacher's Edition
Inquiry Skills Activity Book
Student-Centered Science Activity Books
Program Planning Guide
Guided Reading English Audiotapes
Guided Reading Spanish Audiotapes and Summaries
Product Testing Activities by Consumer Reports™
Event-Based Science Series (NSF funded)
Prentice Hall Interdisciplinary Explorations
Cobblestone, Odyssey, Calliope, and *Faces* Magazines

Media/Technology
Science Explorer Interactive Student Tutorial CD-ROMs
Odyssey of Discovery CD-ROMs
Resource Pro® (Teaching Resources on CD-ROM)
Assessment Resources CD-ROM with Dial-A-Test®
Internet site at www.science-explorer.phschool.com
Life, Earth, and Physical Science Videodiscs
Life, Earth, and Physical Science Videotapes

Science Explorer Student Editions

- *From Bacteria to Plants*
- *Animals*
- *Cells and Heredity*
- *Human Biology and Health*
- *Environmental Science*
- *Inside Earth*
- *Earth's Changing Surface*
- *Earth's Waters*
- *Weather and Climate*
- *Astronomy*
- *Chemical Building Blocks*
- *Chemical Interactions*
- *Motion, Forces, and Energy*
- *Electricity and Magnetism*
- *Sound and Light*

Staff Credits

The people who made up the *Science Explorer* team—representing editorial, editorial services, design services, field marketing, market research, marketing services, on-line services/multimedia development, product marketing, production services, and publishing processes—are listed below. Bold type denotes core team members.

Kristen E. Ball, **Barbara A. Bertell,** Peter W. Brooks, **Christopher R. Brown, Greg Cantone,** Jonathan Cheney, **Patrick Finbarr Connolly,** Loree Franz, Donald P. Gagnon, Jr., **Paul J. Gagnon, Joel Gendler,** Elizabeth Good, Kerri Hoar, **Linda D. Johnson,** Katherine M. Kotik, Russ Lappa, Marilyn Leitao, David Lippman, **Eve Melnechuk, Natania Mlawer,** Paul W. Murphy, **Cindy A. Noftle,** Julia F. Osborne, Caroline M. Power, Suzanne J. Schineller, **Susan W. Tafler,** Kira Thaler-Marbit, Robin L. Santel, Ronald Schachter, **Mark Tricca,** Diane Walsh, Pearl B. Weinstein, Beth Norman Winickoff

Acknowledgment for pages 148–149: "Grandma always made the bread" from *Countryside & Small Stock Journal,* Nov–Dec 1995. Used by permission of the publisher, Countryside Publishing.

ISBN 0-13-434482-0
3 4 5 6 7 8 9 10   03 02 01 00 99

Cover: The chemical reactions of fireworks fill a night sky with color and beauty.

Program Authors

Michael J. Padilla, Ph.D.
Professor
Department of Science Education
University of Georgia
Athens, Georgia

Michael Padilla is a leader in middle school science education. He has served as an editor and elected officer for the National Science Teachers Association. He has been principal investigator of several National Science Foundation and Eisenhower grants and served as a writer of the National Science Education Standards.

As lead author of *Science Explorer,* Mike has inspired the team in developing a program that meets the needs of middle grades students, promotes science inquiry, and is aligned with the National Science Education Standards.

Ioannis Miaoulis, Ph.D.
Dean of Engineering
College of Engineering
Tufts University
Medford, Massachusetts

Martha Cyr, Ph.D.
Director, Engineering
Educational Outreach
College of Engineering
Tufts University
Medford, Massachusetts

Science Explorer was created in collaboration with the College of Engineering at Tufts University. Tufts has an extensive engineering outreach program that uses engineering design and construction to excite and motivate students and teachers in science and technology education.

Faculty from Tufts University participated in the development of *Science Explorer* chapter projects, reviewed the student books for content accuracy, and helped coordinate field testing.

Book Authors

David V. Frank, Ph. D.
Head, Department of Physical Sciences
Ferris State University
Big Rapids, Michigan

John G. Little
Science Teacher
St. Mary's High School
Stockton, California

Steve Miller
Science Writer
State College, Pennsylvania

Contributing Writers

Mary Sue Burns
Science Teacher
Pocahontas County
   High School
Dunmore,
   West Virginia

Peter Kahan
Former Science Teacher
Dwight-Englewood
   School
Englewood,
   New Jersey

Thomas L. Messer
Science Teacher
Cape Cod Academy
Osterville,
   Massachusetts

Linda Shoulberg
Science Teacher
Millbrook High School
Raleigh,
   North Carolina

Thomas R. Wellnitz
Science Teacher
The Paideia School
Atlanta, Georgia

Reading Consultant

Bonnie B. Armbruster, Ph.D.
Department of Curriculum
   and Instruction
University of Illinois
Champaign, Illinois

Interdisciplinary Consultant

Heidi Hayes Jacobs, Ed.D.
Teacher's College
Columbia University
New York, New York

Safety Consultants

W. H. Breazeale, Ph.D.
Department of Chemistry
College of Charleston
Charleston, South Carolina

Ruth Hathaway, Ph.D.
Hathaway Consulting
Cape Girardeau, Missouri

Tufts University Program Reviewers

Behrouz Abedian, Ph.D.
Department of Mechanical
    Engineering

Wayne Chudyk, Ph.D.
Department of Civil and
    Environmental Engineering

Eliana De Bernardez-Clark, Ph.D.
Department of Chemical Engineering

Anne Marie Desmarais, Ph.D.
Department of Civil and
    Environmental Engineering

David L. Kaplan, Ph.D.
Department of Chemical Engineering

Paul Kelley, Ph.D.
Department of Electro-Optics

George S. Mumford, Ph.D.
Professor of Astronomy, Emeritus

Jan A. Pechenik, Ph.D.
Department of Biology

Livia Racz, Ph.D.
Department of Mechanical Engineering

Robert Rifkin, M.D.
School of Medicine

Jack Ridge, Ph.D.
Department of Geology

Chris Swan, Ph.D.
Department of Civil and
    Environmental Engineering

Peter Y. Wong, Ph.D.
Department of Mechanical Engineering

Content Reviewers

Jack W. Beal, Ph.D.
Department of Physics
Fairfield University
Fairfield, Connecticut

W. Russell Blake, Ph.D.
Planetarium Director
Plymouth Community
    Intermediate School
Plymouth, Massachusetts

Howard E. Buhse, Jr., Ph.D.
Department of Biological Sciences
University of Illinois
Chicago, Illinois

Dawn Smith Burgess, Ph.D.
Department of Geophysics
Stanford University
Stanford, California

A. Malcolm Campbell, Ph.D.
Assistant Professor
Davidson College
Davidson, North Carolina

Elizabeth A. De Stasio, Ph.D.
Associate Professor of Biology
Lawrence University
Appleton, Wisconsin

John M. Fowler, Ph.D.
Former Director of Special Projects
National Science Teacher's Association
Arlington, Virginia

Jonathan Gitlin, M.D.
School of Medicine
Washington University
St. Louis, Missouri

Dawn Graff-Haight, Ph.D., CHES
Department of Health, Human
    Performance, and Athletics
Linfield College
McMinnville, Oregon

Deborah L. Gumucio, Ph.D.
Associate Professor
Department of Anatomy and Cell Biology
University of Michigan
Ann Arbor, Michigan

William S. Harwood, Ph.D.
Dean of University Division and Associate
    Professor of Education
Indiana University
Bloomington, Indiana

Cyndy Henzel, Ph.D.
Department of Geography
    and Regional Development
University of Arizona
Tucson, Arizona

Greg Hutton
Science and Health
    Curriculum Coordinator
School Board of Sarasota County
Sarasota, Florida

Susan K. Jacobson, Ph.D.
Department of Wildlife Ecology
    and Conservation
University of Florida
Gainesville, Florida

Judy Jernstedt, Ph.D.
Department of Agronomy and Range Science
University of California, Davis
Davis, California

John L. Kermond, Ph.D.
Office of Global Programs
National Oceanographic and
    Atmospheric Administration
Silver Spring, Maryland

David E. LaHart, Ph.D.
Institute of Science and Public Affairs
Florida State University
Tallahassee, Florida

Joe Leverich, Ph.D.
Department of Biology
St. Louis University
St. Louis, Missouri

Dennis K. Lieu, Ph.D.
Department of Mechanical Engineering
University of California
Berkeley, California

Cynthia J. Moore, Ph.D.
Science Outreach Coordinator
Washington University
St. Louis, Missouri

Joseph M. Moran, Ph.D.
Department of Earth Science
University of Wisconsin–Green Bay
Green Bay, Wisconsin

Joseph Stukey, Ph.D.
Department of Biology
Hope College
Holland, Michigan

Seetha Subramanian
Lexington Community College
University of Kentucky
Lexington, Kentucky

Carl L. Thurman, Ph.D.
Department of Biology
University of Northern Iowa
Cedar Falls, Iowa

Edward D. Walton, Ph.D.
Department of Chemistry
California State Polytechnic University
Pomona, California

Robert S. Young, Ph.D.
Department of Geosciences and
    Natural Resource Management
Western Carolina University
Cullowhee, North Carolina

Edward J. Zalisko, Ph.D.
Department of Biology
Blackburn College
Carlinville, Illinois

Teacher Reviewers

Stephanie Anderson
Sierra Vista Junior
    High School
Canyon Country, California

John W. Anson
Mesa Intermediate School
Palmdale, California

Pamela Arline
Lake Taylor Middle School
Norfolk, Virginia

Lynn Beason
College Station Jr. High School
College Station, Texas

Richard Bothmer
Hollis School District
Hollis, New Hampshire

Jeffrey C. Callister
Newburgh Free Academy
Newburgh, New York

Judy D'Albert
Harvard Day School
Corona Del Mar, California

Betty Scott Dean
Guilford County Schools
McLeansville, North Carolina

Sarah C. Duff
Baltimore City Public Schools
Baltimore, Maryland

Melody Law Ewey
Holmes Junior High School
Davis, California

Sherry L. Fisher
Lake Zurich Middle
    School North
Lake Zurich, Illinois

Melissa Gibbons
Fort Worth ISD
Fort Worth, Texas

Debra J. Goodding
Kraemer Middle School
Placentia, California

Jack Grande
Weber Middle School
Port Washington, New York

Steve Hills
Riverside Middle School
Grand Rapids, Michigan

Carol Ann Lionello
Kraemer Middle School
Placentia, California

Jaime A. Morales
Henry T. Gage Middle School
Huntington Park, California

Patsy Partin
Cameron Middle School
Nashville, Tennessee

Deedra H. Robinson
Newport News Public Schools
Newport News, Virginia

Bonnie Scott
Clack Middle School
Abilene, Texas

Charles M. Sears
Belzer Middle School
Indianapolis, Indiana

Barbara M. Strange
Ferndale Middle School
High Point, North Carolina

Jackie Louise Ulfig
Ford Middle School
Allen, Texas

Kathy Usina
Belzer Middle School
Indianapolis, Indiana

Heidi M. von Oetinger
L'Anse Creuse Public School
Harrison Township, Michigan

Pam Watson
Hill Country Middle School
Austin, Texas

Activity Field Testers

Nicki Bibbo
Russell Street School
Littleton, Massachusetts

Connie Boone
Fletcher Middle School
Jacksonville Beach, Florida

Rose-Marie Botting
Broward County
    School District
Fort Lauderdale, Florida

Colleen Campos
Laredo Middle School
Aurora, Colorado

Elizabeth Chait
W. L. Chenery Middle School
Belmont, Massachusetts

Holly Estes
Hale Middle School
Stow, Massachusetts

Laura Hapgood
Plymouth Community
    Intermediate School
Plymouth, Massachusetts

Sandra M. Harris
Winman Junior High School
Warwick, Rhode Island

Jason Ho
Walter Reed Middle School
Los Angeles, California

Joanne Jackson
Winman Junior High School
Warwick, Rhode Island

Mary F. Lavin
Plymouth Community
    Intermediate School
Plymouth, Massachusetts

James MacNeil, Ph.D.
Concord Public Schools
Concord, Massachusetts

Lauren Magruder
St. Michael's Country
    Day School
Newport, Rhode Island

Jeanne Maurand
Glen Urquhart School
Beverly Farms, Massachusetts

Warren Phillips
Plymouth Community
    Intermediate School
Plymouth, Massachusetts

Carol Pirtle
Hale Middle School
Stow, Massachusetts

Kathleen M. Poe
Kirby-Smith Middle School
Jacksonville, Florida

Cynthia B. Pope
Ruffner Middle School
Norfolk, Virginia

Anne Scammell
Geneva Middle School
Geneva, New York

Karen Riley Sievers
Callanan Middle School
Des Moines, Iowa

David M. Smith
Howard A. Eyer Middle School
Macungie, Pennsylvania

Derek Strohschneider
Plymouth Community
    Intermediate School
Plymouth, Massachusetts

Sallie Teames
Rosemont Middle School
Fort Worth, Texas

Gene Vitale
Parkland Middle School
McHenry, Illinois

Zenovia Young
Meyer Levin Junior
    High School (IS 285)
Brooklyn, New York

PRENTICE HALL
SCIENCE EXPLORER

Contents

Chemical Interactions

Activities

SAVING THE OZONE LAYER

As a child growing up in Mexico, long before he won a Nobel Prize in chemistry, Mario Molina enjoyed playing with science. "I was always interested in chemistry sets or toy microscopes. With the microscope in front of me, I'd take a piece of lettuce, put it in water, and let it rot and really stink. To see the life teeming in a drop of water—that for me was fascinating. Even then I realized it would be great if I could become a research scientist."

What Mario wanted to do, he decided, was "actually use science for things that affect society." Mario Molina began by looking at the chemicals people put into the air.

Dr. Mario Molina Born in Mexico City, chemist Mario Molina is now a Professor of Earth, Atmospheric, and Planetary Sciences at the Massachusetts Institute of Technology in Cambridge, Massachusetts. In 1995, Professor Molina, Sherwood Rowland, and Paul Crutzen won the Nobel Prize in Chemistry for their work on CFCs and the ozone layer.

Cycle of Ozone Destruction

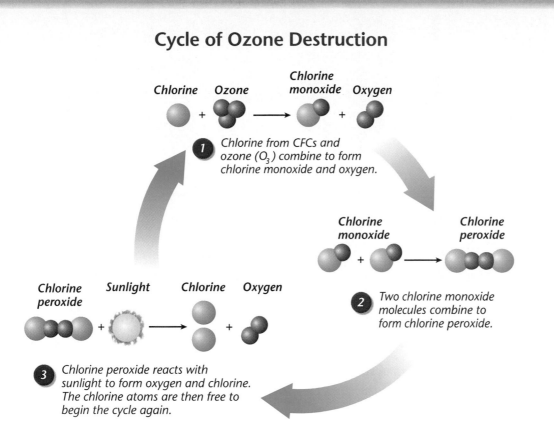

Chlorine   Ozone   Chlorine monoxide   Oxygen

1 Chlorine from CFCs and ozone (O_3) combine to form chlorine monoxide and oxygen.

Chlorine monoxide   Chlorine peroxide

2 Two chlorine monoxide molecules combine to form chlorine peroxide.

Chlorine peroxide   Sunlight   Chlorine   Oxygen

3 Chlorine peroxide reacts with sunlight to form oxygen and chlorine. The chlorine atoms are then free to begin the cycle again.

Asking Simple Questions

In the early 1970s, one of Dr. Molina's co-workers, Sherwood Rowland, heard about a group of compounds called chlorofluorocarbons, or CFCs. CFCs were used in air conditioners, refrigerators, and aerosol spray cans, but leaked into the air. "It is something that is not natural, but is now in the atmosphere all over the planet." What happens to these compounds in the air, Rowland and Molina wondered, and what do they do to the air?

"We didn't know ahead of time if CFCs were doing damage or not," Dr. Molina explains. "So what we did was study what was going on. We learned that CFCs aren't changed much down near Earth. But we expected that if they got high enough in the atmosphere, solar radiation would destroy them."

Radiation is how energy from the sun reaches Earth. Ultraviolet (UV) rays, a form of radiation, break

compounds apart and change them. "Above a certain altitude, everything falls apart. We had to learn how high CFCs went and how long it took them to get there. Then we asked: What does it mean that CFCs are up there?"

A Protective Shield in the Sky

In his laboratory, Dr. Molina studied how ultraviolet light changes CFCs. "It became clear that these molecules would be destroyed by UV rays in the stratosphere—the upper atmosphere, where the ozone layer is. At the time, I didn't even know what the ozone layer was."

But Mario Molina learned fast. The ozone layer is a thin layer of the atmosphere that contains ozone, a form of oxygen. The ozone blocks out UV rays from the sun. UV rays would be dangerous to living things if they reached Earth's surface.

In a 1987 international treaty, the United States and other industrial nations agreed to reduce the use of CFCs in spray cans and other products.

Changes in the ozone layer over Antarctica, 1979 to 1993

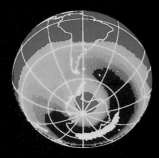

In 1979, thinning of the ozone layer was visible in satellite images.

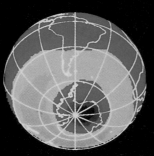

In 1985, a hole in the ozone layer was clearly visible.

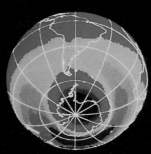

In 1989, the hole in the ozone layer was expanding.

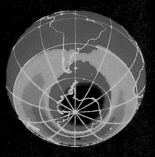

In 1993, the damage to the ozone layer was even worse.

←— Less ozone   More ozone —→

These images of the South Pole, taken by satellite between 1979 and 1993, show a hole developing in the ozone layer of the atmosphere. The changing size and color of the image over the pole represent how quickly the hole increased.

Dr. Molina learned something very disturbing. When the sun's rays break CFCs apart, chlorine forms. A chain of chemical changes that destroys ozone then begins. "Very small amounts of CFCs can have very big effects on ozone."

A Scary Prediction Comes True

Mario Molina and his co-workers made a frightening prediction. If CFCs can reach the stratosphere, they will eventually damage the protective ozone layer. Other scientists thought Mario Molina was wrong or exaggerating. But more and more evidence came in. Researchers sent balloons up into the stratosphere with scientific instruments to measure chlorine formed by CFCs. They found that CFCs were in the stratosphere and that the sun's rays were breaking them down.

Was the ozone layer being hurt? Yes. Over Antarctica, there was an "ozone hole," an opening in the ozone layer. The hole lets in harmful radiation from the sun. "That was a surprise to us and to everybody. It was a very large effect that we hadn't predicted. Some scientists thought the ozone hole was natural, but we thought it was caused by CFCs. We checked it out by doing experiments from Antarctica. In a couple of years it became very clear that this hole was a result of the CFCs."

Scientist and Speaker

Dr. Molina now had to convince people to stop making and using CFCs. "We were lucky that the effect

Shown here is the ER-2 aircraft, which was used to measure gases in the ozone hole over Antarctica. ▶

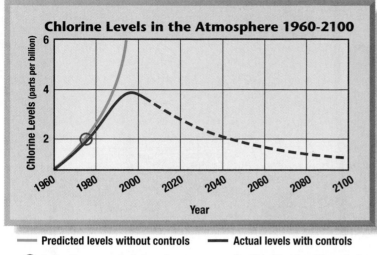

Chlorine Levels in the Atmosphere 1960-2100

Chlorine Levels (parts per billion) vs **Year**

Legend:
— Predicted levels without controls
— Actual levels with controls
○ Antarctica ozone hole found
- - Predicted levels with controls

The graph shows that the level of chlorine in the atmosphere would have increased rapidly if controls on CFCs had not been passed. With controls in place, the amount of chlorine in the atmosphere should gradually decrease to levels in the light blue region of the graph. The ozone hole should then close.

over Antarctica was so large. That made it easy to measure and test. But similar effects exist everywhere. As scientists we had to inform the public and the government. If you're convinced that you're right and that something dangerous is going to happen, you need to risk speaking out."

Mario Molina went to the U.S. Senate and to other governments. He was able to show how UV radiation was causing damage. "There was damage to some crops, damage to growing fish, damage that we can already see and measure today."

Finally, the world listened. Through the United Nations, an agreement was signed by most industrial nations to stop using CFCs by the year 2000.

Work Still to Do

"Everybody has to work together," chemist Molina says. He has done more than his share. He gave $200,000 of his Nobel Prize money to help train scientists from Latin America and other developing countries. "There is a need to understand our planet, and we need very good minds to work on these problems. There are big challenges out there," he says with a confident smile, "but fortunately science is fascinating."

In Your Journal

Mario Molina particularly wants to know how chemicals made by people get into the atmosphere and change it. Take a walk in your neighborhood. Make a list of ways you can observe—or think of—that people put chemicals into the air. Remember that smoke is a mixture of chemicals.

Chemical Reactions

WHAT'S AHEAD

Keep a Chemical Change Log

Look around. All sorts of changes are taking place. Some changes involve growth. For example, you and your classmates are growing. Other changes produce something that wasn't there before. A factory turns raw materials into desirable products, for instance. Rust coats the surface of a once-silvery fence. Even the green color of the Statue of Liberty comes from a change to the statue's copper metal covering. All of these changes are the result of chemistry, or more specifically, of the reactions between two or more chemicals.

In this chapter, you will learn more about the changes in matter that result from chemical reactions. Your project involves keeping a log of chemical changes occurring around you.

Your Goal To identify and observe chemical changes in your daily life and to record evidence for those changes.

To complete the project you must
- ◆ determine what evidence indicates that a chemical change has taken place
- ◆ record observations of the different chemical changes you notice in your life during one week
- ◆ classify the types of chemical changes you observe
- ◆ follow the safety guidelines in Appendix A

Get Started Begin by previewing the chapter to learn what a chemical change is. With a group, discuss some changes you observe regularly. Try to decide if each change is a chemical change.

Check Your Progress You'll be working on this project as you study this chapter. To keep your project on track, look for Check Your Progress boxes at the following points.
Section Review 1, page 21: List evidence of chemical changes.
Section Review 2, page 31: Construct a table for observations.

Wrap Up At the end of the chapter (page 47), you will compare your table of chemical changes with those of your classmates and classify the changes.

Integrating Health 🌐

SECTION
4 Fire and
Fire Safety

Discover How Does Baking Soda Affect a Fire?

The copper-covered
Statue of Liberty has stood
in Upper New York Bay for
over 100 years.

SECTION
① Matter and Its Changes

DISCOVER •• ACTIVITY ••••

What Happens When Chemicals React?

1. Put on your safety goggles.

2. Put 2 teaspoons of baking soda into a clear plastic cup.

3. Holding the cup over a large bowl or sink, add half a cup of vinegar. Swirl the cup gently.

4. Observe any changes to the material in the cup. Feel the outside of the cup. What do you notice about the temperature?

5. Carefully fan some air over the liquid toward you. What does the mixture smell like?

Think It Over

Observing Looking at an experiment is not the only way to get information. Your other senses can be equally useful in making observations. What changes did you detect using your senses of smell and touch?

GUIDE FOR READING

◆ What simple substances make up matter?

◆ How can you tell a chemical reaction has occurred?

◆ How are chemical bonds changed in reactions?

Reading Tip As you read, use the headings of the section to make an outline describing matter and its changes.

A supersonic jet sits on the runway, waiting to fly across the ocean. On a signal from the control tower, the pilot eases the plane forward. Suddenly, there is a rumbling sound. The plane starts to shake and picks up speed. Passengers looking out the window watch the runway zip by as the jet moves faster and faster. Suddenly the jet is off the ground. As the thrust of the engines shoots the plane into the air, the passengers feel as though they are being pushed back into their seats.

The jet's giant engines move matter from one city to another. The jet, its crew and passengers, the baggage, and the jet fuel are all forms of matter. In fact, everything you can see, taste, touch, or smell is matter.

Inside the jet's powerful engines, changes in matter supply the energy needed for the flight. The fuel reacts with oxygen from the air to make new materials and release tremendous amounts of energy. The release of this energy moves the huge jet fast enough to keep it in the air and speeding on its way.

Chemistry is the study of the properties of matter and how matter changes. Some changes are spectacular, like those in the engines that power a jet. Others are as quiet as a cake baking in an oven. But however dramatic a change is, it always involves matter.

◄ Supersonic transport (SST)

Figure 1 A geodesic dome, a bridge, and a skyscraper are all made from steel, but their uses are very different.

Building Blocks of Matter

Take an imaginary walk through your city or town and notice all the buildings. Their shapes, sizes, and uses are very different. You would never confuse a doghouse with an airport terminal or a gas station with a 50-story office tower. But they are all constructed of a few kinds of materials. Bricks, wood, glass, stone, concrete, and steel are some of the most common building materials. Using these materials, people have built many different structures. No two are exactly alike.

Elements Just as many different buildings are made from just a few kinds of materials, all the different kinds of matter in the universe are made from about 100 different substances, called elements. An **element** is a substance that cannot be broken down into any other substances by chemical or physical means.

You have seen some elements in their pure form in the world around you. Examples include aluminum foil, carbon in the form of a graphite pencil lead, copper coatings on pennies, and the tungsten wire that glows in a light bulb. **All the matter around you is composed of one element or a combination of two or more elements.**

Ratios

A ratio compares two numbers. It tells you how much you have of one item in comparison to how much you have of another. For example, a recipe for cookies calls for 2 cups of flour for every 1 cup of sugar. You can write the ratio of flour to sugar as:

2 to 1 or 2 : 1

The elements in a compound are present in a specific ratio. If two compounds contain the same elements in different ratios, they are different compounds.

Compounds Most elements are not found in their pure form in nature. They are more likely found as parts of compounds. A **compound** is a substance made of two or more elements chemically combined in a specific ratio, or proportion. For example, the carbon dioxide gas (CO_2) you breathe out of your lungs is made of carbon atoms and oxygen atoms in a 1 to 2 ratio.

You use many compounds every day. The sugar that makes juice taste sweet, the water you drink when you're thirsty, and the cavity-fighting ingredient in your toothpaste are all compounds made from different combinations of elements.

Sugar, for example, is made of the elements carbon, hydrogen, and oxygen. Think about the white crystals in a sugar bowl. Do they seem much like black powdery carbon and colorless hydrogen and oxygen gases? When elements combine to make compounds, the resulting compound has properties that are different from the elements.

Mixtures Most matter you find in your environment occurs as parts of mixtures. A **mixture** is made from two or more pure substances—elements, compounds, or both—that are in the same place but not combined as a new material. Unlike a compound, the parts of a mixture are not necessarily present in specific ratios. Soil, for example, can be any combination of sand, clay, water, and other materials. Yet it is still soil. Mixtures also differ from compounds because the different parts of the mixture keep their individual properties. You can easily distinguish the many parts of a handful of soil just by looking closely at it.

In some mixtures the individual substances are not easily seen. A **solution** is a well-mixed mixture. If you have ever tasted sea water, you know the salt is there even though you can't see it. But if you let a glass of salt water sit on a sunny windowsill for a few days, the water evaporates and only the salt remains. When the salt and water mix, they are still salt and water. No new materials form.

☑ *Checkpoint* Why can you call elements the building blocks of matter?

Figure 2 Some items in this picture are made of compounds, while others are mixtures. *Applying Concepts What do the compositions of all these items have in common?*

Changes in Matter

Chemistry is not just the study of kinds of matter, but also of how matter changes. Clouds bringing water to your garden, a plant seed, gasoline in a lawn mower engine, a book of matches—all of these are examples of matter. All of them are useful. They are useful as a result of the changes they undergo.

Physical Change Not all changes produce different material. A change that alters the form or appearance of a material but does not make the material into another substance is called a **physical change.**

Figure 3 Matter commonly exists in three different forms, or states. *Interpreting Photographs Name two states of water shown in this photograph. Which state of water is invisible?*

When you think about water in its different forms, you are thinking about physical changes. When it is cooled in a freezer or at the cold regions of Earth, liquid water becomes solid ice. You can change ice to liquid water by leaving an ice cube on your kitchen counter. If it is heated on your stove or by the energy of the sun, liquid water becomes an invisible gas called water vapor. When water vapor becomes liquid again, it returns to the ground as rain. These are all physical changes. Water is still the same substance in all three forms. It is still made of two parts hydrogen and one part oxygen (H_2O).

Chemical Change A change in matter that produces new substances is called a **chemical change.** The new substances are made of the same elements as the original substance, but now in different combinations. Elements and compounds rearrange to make new materials. Elements may combine to make compounds, compounds may be broken down into elements, or compounds may change into other compounds.

Think about elements and compounds as if they were letters and words. Every word is made of specific letters in a certain combination. Likewise, every compound is made of specific elements in a certain combination. A physical change is like printing the same word in a different style of type:

stampedes → *stampedes*

A chemical change, or **chemical reaction,** is like scrambling the letters of a word to make new words:

stampedes → **made** + **steps**

You have seen the results of many chemical reactions. Rusting turns the strong iron metal of a car body into iron oxide, a compound you can easily knock a hole through. When wood burns, the compounds that make up the wood combine with oxygen in the air to make carbon dioxide and water.

☑ *Checkpoint* *How is a physical change different from a chemical change?*

Figure 4 Over time, the surface of a polished bronze statue darkens as it reacts with oxygen in air.

Observing Chemical Reactions

Imagine you are toasting marshmallows over a campfire. You can use your senses to detect chemical changes. You see the burning logs change from a hard solid to a soft pile of ash. You can hear popping and hissing sounds as gases produced by the reaction cause the wood to expand. You can smell the smoke. You can feel the heat energy released. You can even taste the results of one chemical change. A soft, white marshmallow right out of the bag doesn't taste at all like one that is toasted by a reaction of sugar with oxygen.

You can detect many chemical reactions by observing changes in the properties of matter. Such changes result when new substances form. But how can you tell when a new substance is present? Sometimes a gas is produced, which you might see as bubbles in a liquid. Other times, a solid may appear when two solutions are mixed. A solid that forms from solution during a chemical reaction is called a **precipitate** (pree SIP uh tayt). Still other times, a color change or a change in other properties may tell you that a new substance has formed. Changes in energy also happen during reactions, usually indicated by temperature changes. You will learn more about energy and chemical changes in Section 3.

All of these kinds of evidence are good indicators of a chemical reaction. But they may not always be. Sometimes physical changes give similar results. Take, for example, the changes to water described earlier. When water boils, gas bubbles form. When water freezes, solid ice crystals appear. The properties of solid, liquid, and gaseous water differ also. Ice is a hard, sometimes milky white, brittle solid. Liquid water is clear and colorless. Some of the properties differ, but water vapor, ice, and liquid water all are made of hydrogen and oxygen in a 2 to 1 ratio. **The key characteristic of a chemical reaction is the production of new materials that are chemically different from the starting materials.**

Mostly Cloudy

How can you tell if a chemical reaction is taking place?

1. Put on your safety goggles and apron.

2. Pour about 5 mL of lime-water into a plastic cup.

3. Pour an equal amount of plain water into another plastic cup.

4. Add about 5 mL of carbonated water to each of the cups.

Inferring In which cup do you think a chemical reaction occurred? What evidence supports your inference?

EXPLORING Evidence for Chemical Reactions

Chemical reactions produce new substances. The signs of a reaction vary, but many reactions include one or more of the following types of evidence.

Color Change A color change often is a sign that a chemical reaction has occurred. The brilliant colors of fall foliage result when green chlorophyll in leaves breaks down. Then colors of other substances in the leaves become visible.

Precipitation Two clear solutions react when mixed, forming a red precipitate. The presence of the precipitate tells you a chemical change has taken place.

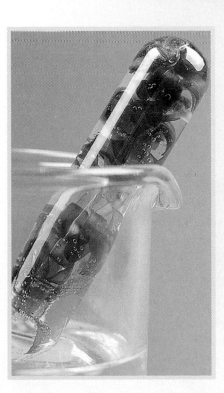

Gas Production Oxygen bubbles formed during photosynthesis collect on the leaves of this underwater plant. Oxygen is a product of the reaction between carbon dioxide and water inside the cells of the plant.

Changes in Temperature The burning of natural gas supplies heat to boil water. An increase or decrease in temperature can result from the changes in energy that happen during a reaction.

Changes in Properties Baking turns flour, water, and other ingredients into light, flaky bread. The loaf of bread with its crunchy crust has very different properties from the soft dough that went into the oven.

Chemical Reactions on a Small Scale

If you walk along a beach, you leave footprints in the sand. Over time, the incoming tide erases them. A beach is constantly changing, as each wave carries new sand in from the ocean and takes some of the shore sand back with it. Sometimes a violent storm can change the outline of a shore in just a few hours, but mostly the beach is changed by wind and water moving sand one tiny grain at a time.

Chemical reactions also occur one small step at a time. When you observe a chemical change, you are watching the combined effect of countless small changes. These changes involve tiny particles of matter.

Atoms and Molecules The matter you see is made of particles you can't see. The smallest particle of an element is an **atom.** All the atoms of an element have the same chemical properties, and these are different from the properties of atoms of other elements. Atoms are unbelievably small. One grain of sand on a beach contains more atoms than there are sand grains on the entire beach!

A **molecule** is the combination of two or more atoms. Some molecules are made of atoms that are all alike, as in the oxygen gas (O_2) that you breathe. Most molecules, though, are made of more than one type of atom. Water molecules have 2 hydrogen atoms combined with 1 oxygen atom (H_2O). Acetic acid, the

Figure 5 The sandy cliffs protecting this lighthouse from the ocean have been worn away as wind and water shifted sand one tiny grain at a time. Moving one piece of sand on a large beach doesn't make a change you can see, but moving billions of pieces changes the shoreline forever.

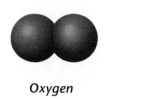
Oxygen

Water

Acetic acid

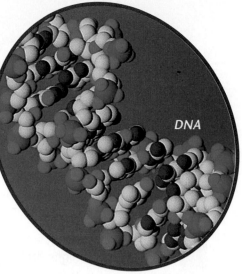
DNA

compound that gives vinegar its sharp odor and sour taste, has 2 carbon atoms, 4 hydrogen atoms, and 2 oxygen atoms ($C_2H_4O_2$). Some of the molecules in your body are made of millions of atoms.

Chemical Bonds and Chemical Reactions   The force that holds atoms together is called a **chemical bond.** You can think of chemical bonds as the "glue" that makes atoms "stick" to each other. The types of atoms and how they are joined by chemical bonds determine the properties of a substance. **Chemical reactions occur when chemical bonds are either formed or broken apart.** When bonds are broken and new ones are formed, atoms are shuffled, making new substances with different properties.

Some chemical bonds are strong and hard to change. Others break apart easily. Glass is unreactive because the chemical bonds that hold it together are strong. Windows in buildings hundreds of years old show no damage from weather, while wood frames around the glass have rotted away. The wood is made of compounds that react easily with other substances in the environment. It can be softened by water and rotted by fungi. Or it can burn in a fire.

Figure 6 Molecules may be as simple as oxygen. Or, they may be as complex as the DNA in living cells. However, all molecules are made of atoms. (The computer image of DNA was made using a color code for atoms different from the code used in this book.)
Classifying Which one of these is a molecule of an element? How do you know?

Section 1 Review

1. Tell how an element, a compound, and a mixture differ.
2. What forms of evidence show that a chemical reaction has taken place?
3. What happens to the chemical bonds in a molecule during a chemical reaction?
4. What is the difference between an atom and a molecule?
5. **Thinking Critically Classifying** Classify the following as chemical or physical changes: ice cream melting; sugar dissolving in water; gasoline burning; a bathroom mirror fogging as someone showers; milk turning sour.

Check Your Progress
CHAPTER PROJECT 1
Use the information from the section to make a list of signs or evidence that a chemical reaction is taking place. Discuss your list with another classmate. (*Hint:* Look outside your home, think about reactions inside your body, and look for reactions that may occur either very slowly or very quickly.) Consider changes you might observe that shouldn't be classified as chemical reactions.

Skills Lab

Where's the Evidence?

Chemical reactions occur all around you. In this lab you will observe different types of evidence of chemical reactions.

Problem

What are some signs that a chemical reaction has taken place?

Materials

4 small plastic cups   birthday candles
2 plastic spoons   sugar
tongs   clay
matches
sodium carbonate (powder)
graduated cylinder, 10 mL
aluminum foil, about 10-cm square
dilute hydrochloric acid in a dropper bottle
copper sulfate solution
sodium carbonate solution

Procedure

Preview the steps for each reaction and copy the data table into your notebook.

Part 1

1. Put a pea-sized pile of sodium carbonate into a clean plastic cup. Record the appearance of the sodium carbonate in the data table.
2. Observe a dropper containing hydrochloric acid. Record the appearance of the acid. **CAUTION:** *Hydrochloric acid can burn you or anything else it touches. Wash spills with water.*
3. Make a prediction about how you think the acid and the sodium carbonate will react when mixed. Record your prediction.
4. Add about 10 drops of hydrochloric acid to the sodium carbonate. Swirl to mix the contents of the cup. Record your observations.

Part 2

5. Fold up the sides of the aluminum foil square to make a small tray.
6. Use a plastic spoon to place a pea-sized pile of sugar into the tray.
7. Carefully describe the appearance of the sugar in your data table.

DATA TABLE				
Reaction	Observations Before Reaction	Predictions	Observations During Reaction	Observations After Reaction
1. Sodium carbonate (powder) + hydrochloric acid				
2. Sugar				
3. Copper sulfate + sodium carbonate solutions				

8. Secure a small candle on your desktop in a lump of clay. Carefully light the candle with a match only after being instructed to do so by your teacher. **CAUTION:** *Tie back long hair and loose clothing.*

9. Predict what you think will happen if you heat the sugar. Record your prediction.

10. Use tongs to hold the aluminum tray. Heat the sugar slowly by moving the tray gently back and forth over the flame. Make observations while the sugar is heating.

11. When you think there is no longer a chemical reaction occurring, blow out the candle.

12. Allow the tray to cool for a few seconds and set it down on your desk. Record your observations of the material left in the tray.

Part 3

13. Put about 2 mL of copper sulfate solution in one cup. **CAUTION:** *Copper sulfate is poisonous and can stain your skin and clothes. Do not touch it or get it in your mouth.* Put an equal amount of sodium carbonate solution in another cup. Record the appearance of both liquids.

14. Predict what you think will happen when the two solutions are mixed. Record your prediction.

15. Combine the two solutions and record your observations. **CAUTION:** *Dispose of the solutions as directed by your teacher.*

16. Wash your hands when you have finished working.

Analyze and Conclude

1. How do the results of each reaction compare with your predictions for that reaction?

2. How did you know when Reaction 1 was over?

3. Was the product of the reaction in Part 1 a solid, a liquid, or a gas? How do you know?

4. How are the properties of the material remaining after the reaction in Part 2 different from those of the sugar?

5. Was the product of the reaction in Part 3 a solid, a liquid, or a gas? How do you know?

6. How do you know if new substances were formed in each reaction?

7. **Think About It** What senses did you use to make observations during this lab? How might you use scientific instruments to extend your senses in order to make more observations?

More to Explore

Use your observation skills to find evidence of chemical reactions involving foods in your kitchen. Look for production of gases, color changes, and formation of precipitates. Share your findings with your classmates.

② Describing Chemical Reactions

DISCOVER • ACTIVITY

Do You Lose Anything?

1. Place about two dozen coins on a table. Sort them into stacks of pennies, nickels, dimes, and quarters.

2. Count and record the number of coins in each stack. Calculate and record the value of each stack and the total of all stacks combined.

3. Mix all the coins together and then divide them randomly into four unsorted stacks.

4. Again calculate the value of each stack and the total amount of money. Count the total number of each type of coin.

5. Repeat Steps 3 and 4.

Think It Over

Making Models What happened to the total value and types of coins in this activity? Did rearranging the coins change any individual coin? If you think of the coins as representing different types of atoms, what does this model tell you about chemical reactions?

GUIDE FOR READING

◆ What does a chemical equation tell you?

◆ How does mass change during a chemical reaction?

◆ What are three categories of chemical reactions?

Reading Tip As you read, describe how each boldfaced vocabulary word relates to a chemical reaction.

Suppose you were to take a walk in a foreign country where the language is unfamiliar to you. Think of the signs you might see—two doors with drawings of a man and a woman, the receiver of a telephone, a drawing of a bicycle, and a picture of a trash can with something dropping into it. You would have no trouble figuring out what these signs mean.

Symbols express a concept in a shorter form. "Hydrogen molecules react with oxygen molecules to form water molecules," is a sentence that describes the reaction between hydrogen and oxygen. But writing it is slow and awkward. A **chemical equation** is a shorter, easier way to show chemical reactions, using symbols instead of words.

Figure 7 Symbols are short and easy-to-recognize ways of saying something. *Inferring* What information does each of these symbols tell you?

Symbols of Common Elements			
Element	**Symbol**	**Element**	**Symbol**
Oxygen	O	Gold	Au
Hydrogen	H	Silver	Ag
Carbon	C	Sulfur	S
Helium	He	Calcium	Ca
Nitrogen	N	Neon	Ne
Chlorine	Cl	Phosphorus	P
Aluminum	Al	Potassium	K
Iron	Fe	Iodine	I
Sodium	Na	Silicon	Si

Figure 8 The symbols for most elements are the first one or two letters of their names. Some elements have symbols that come from their Latin, Greek, or Arabic names.

Writing Chemical Equations

To write a chemical equation, you have to know what chemicals you are starting with and what new chemicals you get during the reaction. Then you can use symbols to stand for the elements and compounds involved.

Chemical Formulas Most elements are represented by a one-letter or two-letter **symbol.** The symbols for some elements that you may recognize are shown in Figure 8. The periodic table in Appendix D shows the symbols for all the elements. Think of these symbols as being like the 26 letters of the alphabet. A compound is represented by a "word," called a **chemical formula,** which shows the ratio of elements in the compound. Figure 9 gives examples of chemical formulas for some common compounds. The chemical formula also may show the number of atoms of each element in one molecule of a compound.

Take the compound hydrogen peroxide, for example. If you look in your medicine cabinet, you might find a bottle. This compound is used to clean cuts and scrapes because it kills bacteria. You can represent hydrogen peroxide by its formula.

$$H_2O_2$$

Notice that the number 2 is lower and smaller than the letter symbols of the elements. This number is called a subscript. A **subscript** shows the number of atoms of an element in a molecule. If a symbol in a chemical formula doesn't have a subscript, the number 1 is understood to be there. Carbon dioxide (CO_2), for example, has one carbon atom and two oxygen atoms. How many atoms in total does a water molecule (H_2O) have? Since the absence of a subscript means that there is one oxygen atom, there are three atoms altogether.

Figure 9 Formulas for compounds tell you what elements as well as how many atoms of each element are present. *Observing How many oxygen atoms are present in water, carbon dioxide, and sugar?*

Formulas of Familiar Compounds	
Compound	**Formula**
Water	H_2O
Carbon dioxide	CO_2
Carbon monoxide	CO
Natural gas	CH_4
Propane	C_3H_8
Sugar	$C_{12}H_{22}O_{11}$
Rubbing alcohol	C_3H_8O
Ammonia	NH_3
Sodium chloride	NaCl
Washing soda	Na_2CO_3
Baking soda	$NaHCO_3$

Structure of an Equation

Structure of an Equation A chemical equation summarizes the changes in a reaction. It tells you the substances you start with and the substances you get at the end. The materials you have at the beginning are the **reactants.** When the reaction is complete, you have different materials, called the **products** of the reaction.

Chemical equations have a definite structure. **A chemical equation uses symbols to show the reactants and products of a chemical reaction.** The formulas for all the reactants are written on the left side of the equation, and the formulas for all the products are on the right:

$$Reactant + Reactant \rightarrow Product + Product$$

You read the arrow ($\rightarrow$) as "yields." The number of reactants and products can vary. Some reactions have only one reactant or product. Other reactions have three or more reactants or products. Look at the equation for a reaction that forms hydrogen peroxide and count the number of reactants:

$$\underset{Reactant}{H_2} \quad + \quad \underset{Reactant}{O_2} \quad \rightarrow \quad \underset{Product}{H_2O_2}$$

Conservation of Mass

No matter how many reactants and products are involved, all the atoms present at the start of a reaction are present at the end. Think about what happens when classes change at your school. A group of students and a teacher together in one room is called a class. When the bell rings, people move from room to room, ending up in different groups. The number of students and teachers in the school has not changed. But their arrangement is different and the new groups interact differently.

Figure 10 When iron filings and sulfur are mixed and heated, the product is the compound iron sulfide. *Interpreting Diagrams How do you know that mass has been conserved in the reaction?*

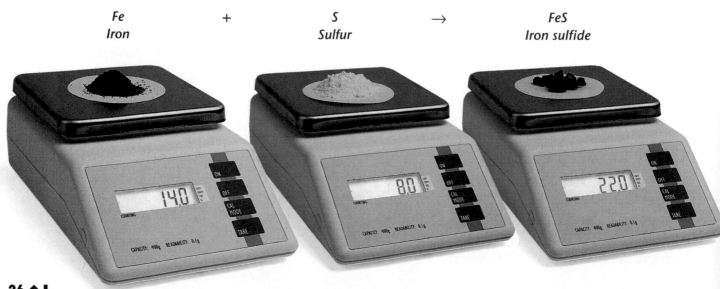

| Fe | + | S | $\rightarrow$ | FeS |
| Iron | | Sulfur | | Iron sulfide |

Figure 11 Burnt wood and gray ash are all that remain from a roaring fire.
Problem Solving When wood burns, it reacts with oxygen in the air. What masses would you need to measure before and after the fire to show conservation of mass?

Now imagine that all the students and teachers are atoms, and each class is a molecule. At the end of a reaction (similar to a class change), the same atoms exist, but they are grouped together in different molecules. **The amount of matter in a chemical reaction does not change, so the total mass of the reactants must equal the total mass of the products.** This principle, called the **conservation of mass,** states that during a chemical reaction, matter is not created or destroyed.

At first glance, some reactions seem to violate the principle of conservation of mass. If you measured the cooled ash left from a wood fire, for example, it wouldn't have the same mass as the wood that had been burned. What happened to the missing mass? Much of it escapes into the air as carbon dioxide gas and water vapor. If you could trap and measure these gases, you'd be able to prove this.

☑ *Checkpoint* How do the numbers and masses of the atoms in the reactants of a chemical reaction compare with the atoms in the products?

Balancing Chemical Equations

What does the principle of conservation of mass mean for a chemical equation? Matter is not created or destroyed in a reaction. This means that the same atoms exist in the products as in the reactants. To accurately describe a reaction, a chemical equation must show the same number of each type of atom on both sides of the equation. When it does, chemists say the equation is balanced. Look at the following statement:

Oxygen reacts with hydrogen to form water.

This statement doesn't tell you everything you need to know. How many atoms does an oxygen molecule have? How about hydrogen? What is the formula for water?

Still There

Use nuts and bolts to model the principle of conservation of mass.

1. Measure the mass of a collection of bolts, each with a nut attached to it.

2. Remove all the nuts from the bolts. Measure the total mass of the nuts. Then do the same with the bolts. Add these values.

3. Rearrange your collection, putting two or three nuts on one bolt, one nut on another bolt, and so on. You can even leave a few pieces unattached.

4. Measure the total mass again. Compare this figure with the totals from Steps 1 and 2.

Making Models How are the nuts and bolts similar to atoms and molecules in a chemical reaction? How do your observations model conservation of mass?

Calculating ACTIVITY

Each chemical formula below is written just as it might be in a balanced chemical equation. For each formula, calculate the number of each kind of atom.

3 H₂O
2 H₂SO₄
4 Fe₂O₃
6 NaCl
NO₂

When a coefficient is in front of a formula, how do you find the total number of atoms of one kind? What do you do if there is no coefficient?

Look at the chemical equation and models for the reaction:

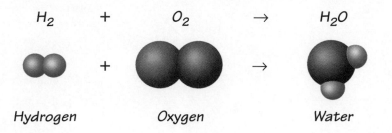

That's better. But if you count the number of atoms of each element in this equation, you find 2 atoms of oxygen in the reactants and only 1 atom of oxygen in the products.

How can you get the number of oxygen molecules on both sides to be the same? You might be tempted to balance the oxygen by changing the formula for water to H_2O_2. Don't even think about it! Remember that H_2O_2 is the formula for hydrogen peroxide, a completely different compound.

To balance the equation, use a coefficient. A **coefficient** (koh uh FISH unt) is a number *in front of* a chemical formula in the equation. It tells you how many molecules or atoms of each reactant and product take part in the reaction. If the coefficient is 1, you don't need to write it. Balance the chemical equation by changing the coefficient for water to 2. It's like saying "2 × H_2O." Now there are 2 oxygen atoms in the product.

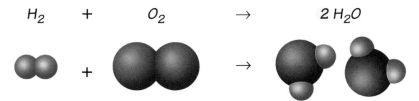

Okay, you've balanced the oxygen atoms. But now there are 2 hydrogen atoms in the reactants and 4 in the product. How can you balance the hydrogen? Try doubling the number of hydrogen atoms on the left side of the equation by changing the coefficient for hydrogen to 2. You've got it! Here is the balanced equation:

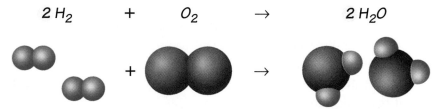

Now there are 4 hydrogen atoms and 2 oxygen atoms on each side. The equation is balanced. It tells you that 2 molecules of hydrogen react with 1 molecule of oxygen to yield 2 molecules of water. Count the atoms in the last diagram. Prove to yourself that the balanced equation is correct.

Sample Problem

When magnesium metal, Mg, reacts with oxygen, O_2, the product of the reaction is magnesium oxide, MgO. Write a balanced equation for this reaction.

Write the word equation.	Magnesium + Oxygen → Magnesium oxide
Write the chemical equation.	Mg + O_2 → MgO
Count the number of atoms of each element on each side of the equation.	Mg O Mg O one two one one
Choose coefficients to balance the equation.	$2\,Mg$ + O_2 → $2\,MgO$
Think about it.	The answer shows 2 magnesium atoms and 2 oxygen atoms on each side, so the equation is balanced.

Practice Problems

1. Balance the equation: $C + Cl_2 \rightarrow CCl_4$
2. Balance the equation: $Al_2O_3 \rightarrow Al + O_2$

Classifying Chemical Reactions

Chemical reactions can be classified by what happens to the reactants and products. Substances may add together to make a more complex substance. They may break apart to make simpler substances or even exchange parts with something else. In each case, new materials form. **Many chemical reactions can be classified in one of three categories: synthesis, decomposition, or replacement.** As you read about each of these kinds of reactions, look at the examples. Compare the reactants and the products to see how they change.

Synthesis Have you ever listened to music from a synthesizer? You can hear many different notes and types of musical sounds. The synthesizer combines these sounds to make a complicated piece of music. When two or more substances (elements or compounds) combine to make a more complex substance, the process is called a **synthesis** (SIN thuh sis) reaction. To synthesize is to put things together. Look back at the reaction of hydrogen and oxygen to make water. You should see now that this is a synthesis reaction—two elements come together, making a compound.

Figure 12 When a ribbon of magnesium metal burns in air (left), it combines with oxygen to form magnesium oxide (right). The shiny metal and colorless gas become a white powdery solid. *Classifying* Why is this a synthesis reaction?

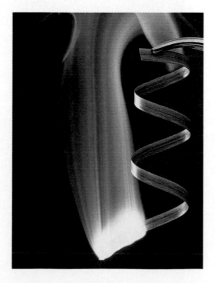

Acid rain is a product of synthesis reactions. In one case, sulfur dioxide, oxygen, and water combine to make sulfuric acid. This is the equation for the reaction:

$$2\,SO_2 \quad + \quad O_2 \quad + \quad 2\,H_2O \quad \rightarrow \quad 2\,H_2SO_4$$
Sulfur dioxide   Oxygen   Water   Sulfuric acid

Sulfur dioxide comes from car engines or from power plants that burn coal. Oxygen and water vapor are in the air. Together they produce sulfuric acid, which causes rainwater to become corrosive. This acid water then eats away at stone and metal, and can damage living organisms. (Can you find the 8 oxygen atoms on each side of the equation?)

Decomposition While a synthesis reaction builds compounds from simpler reactants, a **decomposition** reaction breaks down compounds into simpler products. Remember the bottle of hydrogen peroxide used to clean cuts? If you keep such a bottle for a very long time, you'll have water instead. The hydrogen peroxide decomposes into water and oxygen gas.

$$2\,H_2O_2 \rightarrow 2\,H_2O + O_2$$

The oxygen produced escapes into the air.

☑ *Checkpoint* *How do synthesis and decomposition reactions differ?*

Figure 13 Safety airbags in cars inflate as a result of a decomposition reaction. On impact, a detonator cap inside the air bag explodes. The explosion causes a compound made of sodium and nitrogen to decompose. One product is a large quantity of nitrogen gas.
Applying Concepts Why would quick inflation of airbags be important?

Replacement A reaction in which one element replaces another in a compound, or in which two elements in different compounds trade places, is called a **replacement reaction.** Pure copper metal, for example, is obtained by heating rock containing copper oxide in the presence of charcoal. The carbon of the charcoal takes the place of copper in the copper oxide. You can write the reaction as:

$$2\ CuO + C \rightarrow 2\ Cu + CO_2$$

Obtaining copper metal from rock is a simple replacement reaction. However, not all chemical reactions can be classified clearly as synthesis, decomposition, or replacement. Look carefully at the formulas of the reactants and products for clues to what type of reaction the equation shows.

Figure 14 Copper metal can be chemically obtained from copper ore. Copper oxide (in the ore) reacts with carbon in a replacement reaction.

Section 2 Review

1. What information do you need in order to write a chemical equation?
2. What is the principle of conservation of mass?
3. List and define three categories of chemical reactions.
4. **Thinking Critically Applying Concepts** Balance the following chemical equations by adding coefficients:
   a. $HCl + NaOH \rightarrow H_2O + NaCl$
   b. $Fe_2O_3 + C \rightarrow Fe + CO_2$
   c. $SO_2 + O_2 \rightarrow SO_3$
5. **Thinking Critically Classifying** Classify each of the following reactions as synthesis, decomposition, or replacement:
   a. $2\ NH_4NO_3 \rightarrow 2\ N_2 + O_2 + 4\ H_2O$
   b. $2\ Al + Fe_2O_3 \rightarrow Al_2O_3 + 2\ Fe$
   c. $MgCl_2 + K_2S \rightarrow MgS + 2\ KCl$
   d. $P_4O_{10} + 6\ H_2O \rightarrow 4\ H_3PO_4$

CHAPTER PROJECT 1

Check Your Progress
Prepare a table to keep track of the chemical changes you observe. Have your teacher check your table to be sure it contains the proper headings. Record the different chemical changes you observe for a week. Make sure you can describe the evidence for each chemical change. If possible, classify each reaction as a synthesis, decomposition, or replacement reaction. Also classify it as occurring in a living or nonliving setting.

SECTION 3 Controlling Chemical Reactions

DISCOVER 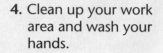 ACTIVITY

Can You Speed Up or Slow Down a Reaction?

1. Put on your safety goggles and lab apron.

2. ▢ Obtain about half a cup each of three solutions of vitamin C and water—one at room temperature, one at about 75°C, and one chilled to between 5° and 10°C.

3. ☠ Add three drops of iodine solution to each container and stir each with a clean spoon. Compare changes you observe in the solutions.

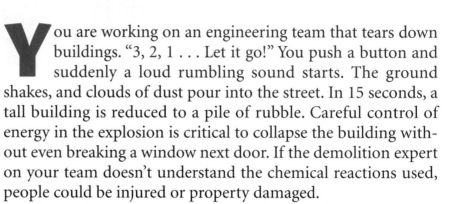

4. Clean up your work area and wash your hands.

Think It Over

Inferring What conclusion can you make about the effect of temperature on the reaction of iodine and vitamin C?

GUIDE FOR READING

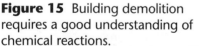

◆ How is energy related to chemical reactions?

◆ How can you control the rate of a chemical reaction?

Reading Tip As you read, make a list of factors affecting reaction rate.

Figure 15 Building demolition requires a good understanding of chemical reactions.

You are working on an engineering team that tears down buildings. "3, 2, 1 . . . Let it go!" You push a button and suddenly a loud rumbling sound starts. The ground shakes, and clouds of dust pour into the street. In 15 seconds, a tall building is reduced to a pile of rubble. Careful control of energy in the explosion is critical to collapse the building without even breaking a window next door. If the demolition expert on your team doesn't understand the chemical reactions used, people could be injured or property damaged.

Although you may never demolish a building, you do use energy from controlled chemical reactions every day. Every time you convert your lunch into the energy to play sports or go for a ride in a car, you are using controlled reactions.

Energy in Chemical Reactions

Light is a type of energy. Other forms of energy include electricity and the energy of a moving object. **Every chemical reaction involves a change of energy. Some reactions release energy and others absorb energy.**

The reaction between gasoline and oxygen in a car engine yields carbon dioxide, water, and other products. It also releases a lot of energy. You can detect one form of this energy as heat. The engine of a car gets hot enough to burn you if you touch it. A reaction that releases energy in the form of heat is called an **exothermic reaction** (ek soh THUR mik).

If you did the Discover activity in Section 1, you observed that the mixture became colder. When baking soda (sodium bicarbonate) reacts with vinegar, the reaction takes heat from the solution, making it feel cooler. This kind of reaction, which absorbs energy, is called an **endothermic reaction** (en doh THUR mik).

Figure 17 compares the changes in energy of exothermic and endothermic reactions. Notice that the energy of the products in an exothermic reaction is lower than the energy of the reactants. In an exothermic reaction, energy is released. This is the case when gasoline burns. Now see how the diagram for an endothermic reaction is different. In an endothermic reaction, the energy of the products is greater than the energy of the reactants, which means energy is absorbed. That's what happened with the baking soda and vinegar.

Figure 16 The endothermic reaction inside a cold pack helps cool this boy's injured ankle. Such rapid treatment after an injury reduces pain and speeds up healing.

Getting Reactions Started

Trace each diagram in Figure 17 from left to right with your finger. As your finger moves, do you notice how the curve goes up and over a rise? Then your finger moves down toward the products. All chemical reactions need energy to get started. The **activation energy** is the minimum amount of energy that has to be added to start a reaction.

Figure 17 Chemical reactions include changes in energy. *Interpreting Diagrams Tell where increases and decreases in energy are shown in each diagram.*

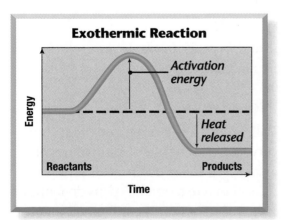

Exothermic Reaction

Energy

Activation energy

Heat released

Reactants   Products

Time

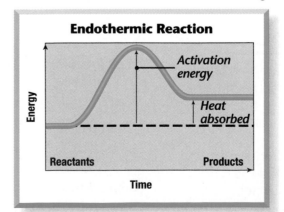

Endothermic Reaction

Energy

Activation energy

Heat absorbed

Reactants   Products

Time

Figure 18 The rock at the top of this hill cannot roll down the hill until a small push gets it going.

Social Studies
CONNECTION

In the early part of the 1900s, people sometimes traveled in airships called dirigibles. Unlike modern airships, which are filled with unreactive helium, some dirigibles contained flammable hydrogen. On May 6, 1937, the airship *Hindenburg* came in for a landing over Lakehurst, New Jersey. Somehow the ship caught fire. Seconds later, its 200,000 cubic meters of hydrogen gas burst into flame, killing 36 people. The *Hindenburg* was a tragic example of how much energy could be released by a reaction between hydrogen and oxygen.

In Your Journal

Pretend you are a reporter covering the scene of the disaster. Write a brief news article explaining to your readers how the reaction between hydrogen and oxygen affected the *Hindenberg* disaster.

The reaction that makes water from hydrogen and oxygen is very exothermic. It gives off tremendous amounts of energy. But if you make a mixture of hydrogen and oxygen, it could remain for years without any noticeable change. However, all it would take to ignite a tiny amount of hydrogen is an electric spark. The spark is a source of activation energy. After the first few molecules react, the large amount of energy released provides the activation energy for more molecules to react.

Think of a chemical reaction as being like a rock resting behind a ridge at the top of a hill. The rock stays put until someone or something adds energy by giving it a push. With enough energy, the rock can move over the hump and roll down the hill. The same idea applies to a chemical reaction. With enough energy, reactants can get "over the hump" and form products.

It's not always clear where the energy to start a reaction comes from. In the case of vinegar and baking soda, heat already in the solution provides the energy to get the reaction started. This reaction is endothermic. To keep going, more energy is continually drawn from the solution. As a result, the mixture gets cooler.

☑ *Checkpoint* *What's the difference between an endothermic reaction and an exothermic reaction?*

Rates of Chemical Reactions

Chemical reactions don't all occur at the same rate. Some reactions, like explosions, are very fast. Others, like rusting of metal, are much slower. Even similar reactions can occur at different rates depending on conditions. How fast a reaction happens depends on how easily the particles of the reactants can get together.

If you want to make a reaction happen faster, you need to get more particles of the reactants together more often. To slow down a reaction, you need to do the opposite—get fewer particles together less often. Chemists do this by controlling the conditions of a reaction. **The rate of a reaction is affected by such factors as concentration, surface area, and temperature.**

Figure 19 Bubbles of hydrogen form when magnesium reacts with an acid. The test tube on the left has a lower concentration of acid than the test tube on the right. *Relating Cause and Effect How does the concentration of acid affect the rate of the reaction?*

Concentration One way to increase the rate of a reaction is to increase the concentration of the reactants. **Concentration** is the amount of one material in a given volume of another material. For example, a teaspoon of sugar in a glass of lemonade will make it sweet. But a tablespoon of sugar in the glass makes the lemonade a lot sweeter! The glass of lemonade with more sugar has a greater concentration of sugar molecules.

Increasing the concentration of reactants makes more particles available to react. Compare the test tubes in Figure 19. A greater concentration of acid in the right test tube means more acid is present to react with the magnesium metal. You can see how the increase in the rate of reaction increases the number of bubbles.

Surface Area When a solid reacts with a liquid or a gas, only particles that are on the surface of the solid come in contact with the other reactant. Now suppose you break the solid into smaller pieces. What happens? You've increased the surface area of the

Figure 20 The concrete walls of this grain elevator in Kansas were blown apart by an explosion when grain particles and oxygen above the stored wheat exploded. Grain dust has a much greater surface area exposed to air than the top surface of a pile of grain does.

Interpreting Data

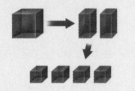

1. Measure the length and width of a face of a gelatin cube.

2. Calculate the area of that face of the cube.
   Area = length × width
   Repeat for each of the other five faces. Then add the six values together to get the total surface area.

3. Using a plastic knife, cut the cube in half and repeat Steps 1 and 2 for each piece of gelatin. Add the surface areas of the two pieces to get the new total surface area.

4. How did the total surface area of the cube before it was cut compare with the total surface area after it was cut?

5. Predict what would happen to the total surface area if you cut each cube in two again. If you have time, test your prediction.

solid. More material is exposed, so the reaction happens faster. Imagine how hard it would be for your body to digest food if you didn't chew it. By chewing, you break the food into smaller pieces. Then your digestive juices can work more quickly to change the food into nutrients your body can use.

Temperature A third way to increase the rate of a reaction is to add heat. When you heat something, its particles move faster. Faster-moving particles increase the reaction rate in two ways. First, they come in contact more often, which means there are more chances for a reaction to happen. Second, faster-moving particles have more energy. This energy helps the reactants get over the activation energy hump.

Did you ever leave a glass of milk out on the kitchen counter when you left for school? When you picked it up again later, the milk may have had a sour smell. When foods are left unrefrigerated, bacteria in them reproduce quickly. As they live and reproduce, the bacteria carry out thousands of chemical reactions. Some reactions can cause food to spoil. Keeping foods cold slows these reactions and the growth of the organisms that cause them. Your food stays fresh longer.

Catalysts Another way to control the rate of a reaction is to change the activation energy. If you decrease the activation energy, the reaction happens faster. A **catalyst** (KAT uh list) is a material that increases the rate of a reaction by lowering the activation energy. Catalysts help with the reaction, but they are not reactants themselves. Catalysts are not permanently changed in the reaction.

Figure 21 Unrefrigerated foods quickly spoil from the chemical reactions carried out by microorganisms. Keeping foods cold slows these changes.

INTEGRATING LIFE SCIENCE Many chemical reactions happen at temperatures that would be deadly to living things. Yet, some of these reactions are necessary for life. The cells in your body (as in all living things) contain biological catalysts called **enzymes** (EN zymz). Enzymes provide a surface on which reactions take place. This helps reactions happen at lower temperatures because it lowers activation energy. In this way, enzymes safely increase the reaction rates of chemical reactions necessary for life. An enzyme breaks away unchanged at the end of a reaction.

Inhibitors Sometimes a reaction is more useful when it can be slowed down rather than speeded up. A material used to decrease the rate of a reaction is called an **inhibitor.**

The discovery of one inhibitor had an important effect on the construction industry. Nitroglycerin is a powerful liquid explosive that decomposes quickly, releasing tremendous energy. An explosion can be caused just by shaking the bottle! In the 1860s, Alfred Nobel tried adding certain solid materials, such as wood pulp, to the nitroglycerin. The solids absorbed the liquid and kept it from reacting until it was ignited. This mixture could be handled more safely and still be used for blasting. Nobel's discovery is the more easily controlled material known as dynamite.

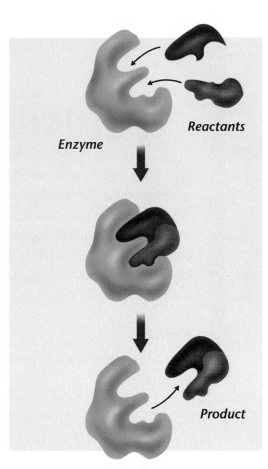

Figure 22 Enzyme molecules are shaped in ways that help reactant molecules come together.

Section 3 Review

1. Compare the change of energy in an exothermic reaction to that in an endothermic reaction.
2. Describe three ways to increase the rate of a chemical reaction.
3. Which has greater surface area: a sugar cube or an equal mass of sugar crystals? Explain.
4. **Thinking Critically Relating Cause and Effect** Copy and complete the table below to show how some factors increase, decrease, or have no effect on rate of a reaction and activation energy.

Changes	Reaction Rate	Activation Energy
Decreased concentration		
Increased surface area		
Heat added		
Catalyst		

Science at Home

Place an iron nail in a plastic cup. Add enough water to almost cover the nail. Place a small piece of fine steel wool in another cup and add the same amount of water. Ask family members to predict what will happen if the nail and steel wool are left overnight. The next day, examine the nail and steel wool. Compare the amount of rust on each. Were your family's predictions correct? Explain how the rate of a reaction depends on the different surface areas of the steel wool and the nail.

Real-World Lab

Peroxide, Catalase, & You!

Hydrogen peroxide is a poisonous waste product of reactions in living cells. An enzyme called catalase, found in the blood, speeds up the breakdown of hydrogen peroxide into harmless water and oxygen gas. In this lab, you will explore the action of catalase under changing conditions.

Problem

How does temperature affect the action of an enzyme?

Skills Focus

measuring, controlling variables, drawing conclusions

Materials

test tube with a one-hole stopper
0.1% hydrogen peroxide solution
forceps
filter paper disks soaked in liver preparation (catalase enzyme) and kept at four different temperatures (room temperature, 0–4°C, 37°C, and 100°C)
container to hold water (beaker or bowl)
stopwatch

Procedure

1. Form a hypothesis that predicts how the action of the catalase enzyme will differ at the different temperatures to be tested.
2. Fill a container with water. Then fill a test tube with 0.1% hydrogen peroxide solution until the test tube is overflowing. Do this over a sink or the container of water.
3. Make a data table similar to the one shown.

DATA TABLE

Temperature (°C)	Time (sec)	Average Time for Class (sec)

4. Moisten the small end of a one-hole stopper with water.

5. Using forceps, remove a filter paper disk soaked in liver preparation (catalase enzyme) that has been kept at room temperature. Stick it to the moistened end of the one-hole stopper.

6. Your partner should be ready with the stopwatch for the next step.

7. Place the stopper firmly into the test tube, hold your thumb over the hole, and quickly invert the test tube. Start the stopwatch. Put the inverted end of the test tube into the container of water, as shown in the photograph, and remove your thumb.

8. Observe what happens to the filter paper inside the test tube. Record the time it takes for the disk to rise to the top. If the disk does not rise within 2 minutes, record "no reaction" and go on to Step 9.

9. Rinse the test tube and repeat the procedure with catalase enzyme disks kept at 0°C, 37°C, and 100°C. **CAUTION:** *When you remove the disk kept in the hot water bath, do not use your bare hands. Avoid spilling the hot water.*

Analyze and Conclude

1. What makes the disk float to the top of the test tube?

2. Calculate the average time for each temperature based on the results of the entire class. Enter the results in your data table.

3. Make a line graph of the data you collected. Label the horizontal axis (*x*-axis) "Temperature" with a scale from 0°C to 100°C. Label the vertical axis (*y*-axis) "Time" with a scale from 0 to 120 seconds. Plot the class average time for each temperature.

4. What evidence do you have that your hypothesis from Step 1 is either supported or not supported?

5. How is the time it takes the disk to rise to the top of the tube related to the rate of the reaction?

6. What can you conclude about the activity of the enzyme at the various temperatures you tested? (*Hint:* Enzyme activity is greater when the rate of reaction is faster.)

7. Make a prediction about how active the enzyme would be at 10°C, 60°C, and 75°C. Give reasons to support your prediction.

8. **Apply** Oxygen kills many kinds of bacteria that can cause infection. Explain why hydrogen peroxide is often used as a treatment on cuts and scrapes.

Design an Experiment

The activity of an enzyme also depends upon the concentration of the enzyme. Design an experiment that explores the relationship between enzyme activity and enzyme concentration. (Your teacher can give you disks soaked with different enzyme concentrations.)

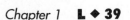

SECTION 4 Fire and Fire Safety

DISCOVER •••••••••••••••••••••••••••••••• ACTIVITY

How Does Baking Soda Affect a Fire?

1. Put on your safety goggles.

2. Secure a small candle in a holder or some clay. After instructions from your teacher, use a match to light the candle.

3. Place a beaker or glass next to the candle. Measure one tablespoon of baking soda into the beaker. Add 1/4 cup of water and stir. Add 1/4 cup of vinegar.

4. As soon as the mixture stops foaming, tip the beaker as if you are pouring something out of it onto the flame. **CAUTION:** *Do not pour any liquid on the candle.*

5. Observe what happens to the flame.

Think It Over

Developing Hypotheses The gas produced in the beaker was carbon dioxide. Based on the results of this experiment, develop a hypothesis to explain what you observed in Step 5.

GUIDE FOR READING

◆ What are the three things necessary to maintain a fire?

◆ How does water stop combustion?

Reading Tip Before you read, predict what conditions contribute to the start of a fire. Revise your predictions as you read.

What picture comes to mind when you hear the word *fire?* Do you think of a warm campfire on a cold night or a house reduced to a pile of ashes? All fires are chemically similar, but a fire can be useful or disastrous depending on whether or not it is controlled. You can keep fires under control, but only if you understand fire as a chemical reaction.

Understanding Fire

Fire is the result of **combustion,** a rapid reaction between oxygen and a substance called a fuel. A **fuel** is a material that releases energy when it burns. Some fuels you probably know about are oil, coal, wood, gasoline, and paper. Combustion of these types of fuel always produces carbon dioxide and water. Sometimes products such as smoke and poisonous gases may form from incomplete combustion or the presence of other materials.

The Fire Triangle Although a combustion reaction is very exothermic and fast, a fire cannot start unless conditions are right. **Three things are necessary to start and maintain a fire—fuel, oxygen, and heat.**

Where does oxygen come from? You probably know the answer is the air. About 20 percent of the air around you is composed of oxygen gas. If air can reach the fuel, so can oxygen. A large fire can actually draw oxygen toward it. As other gases in the air around the flame are heated, they move rapidly away from the fire. Cooler air flows toward the fire, bringing a fresh supply of oxygen. If you stand in front of a fire in a fireplace, you can often feel the flow of air to the fire.

The third part of the fire triangle is heat. Fuel and oxygen can be together, but they won't react until something provides enough activation energy to start the combustion reaction. This energy can come from a lighted match, an electric spark, lightning, or the heat from a stove. Once the reaction starts, the heat released by the combustion can keep the reaction going.

Once a fire has started, it can continue a long time, as long as all three components of the fire triangle are available. Coal in abandoned mines underneath the town of Centralia, Pennsylvania, started burning in 1962 and continues to burn. Many old ventilation shafts lead into the tunnels, but they have never been mapped. Since all the shafts cannot be located and sealed, air (containing oxygen) continues to flow into the mines, supporting the fire. Heat and poisonous gases coming up from the fire through cracks in the ground made living in Centralia difficult. Everyone eventually moved away. No one knows how long this fire will continue to burn.

✓ *Checkpoint* *What is necesssary to start a fire?*

Controlling Fire Use your knowledge of chemical reactions to think of ways to control a fire. What if you remove one part of the fire triangle? For example, you can get the fuel away from the flames. You can also keep oxygen from getting to the fuel, or cool the combustion reaction below its activation energy. Any of these actions may help bring a fire under control.

Think about how firefighters put out a fire in a building. They use large hoses to spray huge amounts of water on the flaming part of the building.

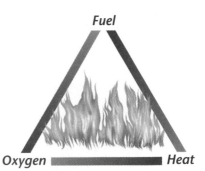

Figure 23 If any point of the fire triangle is missing, a fire will not continue. *Applying Concepts How does putting a lid over a burning pot of food affect the fire triangle?*

Figure 24 Firefighters use water to cool a fire and prevent oxygen from reaching the fuel.

Water removes two parts of the fire triangle. First, water covers the fuel, which keeps it from coming into contact with oxygen. Second, evaporation of the water uses a large amount of heat, causing the fire to cool. Without heat, there isn't enough energy to reach the activation energy of combustion, so the reaction stops.

Home Fire Safety

Every year, fire claims thousands of lives in the United States. If you know how to prevent fires in your home and what to do if a fire starts, you are better prepared to take action. You may save your home or even your life!

Common Sources of Fires The two most common sources of home fires are small heaters and fires that start in the kitchen during cooking. Another common cause is faulty electrical wiring. The fires that cause the most deaths start from carelessness with cigarettes.

Fighting Fires You can fight a small fire by using what you know about the fire triangle. For example, carbon dioxide gas can be used to smother a fire by preventing contact between the fuel and oxygen in the air. If a small fire should start on the stove,

Figure 25 Families can take several steps to prevent fire and to be ready for action if one should start. *Making Judgments Which of these fire safety aids do you think are most important for a home to have?*

Fire Safety Tips

◆ Keep matches and other sources of flames away from young children.

◆ Replace frayed or broken electric cords, and repair appliances that aren't working right.

◆ Keep flammable things, like potholders, towels, and curtains, away from stove burners.

◆ Store gasoline outside the home and only in a safety can.

◆ Never use a gas or charcoal grill inside the home.

◆ Keep a box of baking soda in the kitchen to fight grease fires.

◆ Have at least one fire extinguisher in good working order and within easy reach in your home.

◆ Most importantly, make sure there is a working smoke detector on every level of your home. Check it regularly.

covering it with baking soda may put the fire out. Liquids in food will react with baking soda to produce carbon dioxide. The baking soda itself will help smother the fire, too.

The smaller a fire is, the easier it is to control. You can cool a match enough to stop combustion just by blowing on it. A small fire in a trash can may be doused with a pan of water. If the fire spreads to the curtains, however, even a garden hose might not deliver enough water to put it out.

One of the most effective ways to fight a small fire is with a fire extinguisher. Extinguishers designed for home use are effective when used properly. But a fire that is growing as you fight it is out of control. If this happens, there is only one safe thing to do—get away from the fire and let the fire department handle it.

Preventing Trouble The best form of fire safety is fire prevention. With your family, check your home for fire hazards and firefighting aids. Look at the list on the opposite page for some things you and your family can do.

Fires can be dangerous and deadly, but many fires can be prevented if you are careful. Understanding the chemistry of fire gives you a way to reduce risk and increase your family's safety.

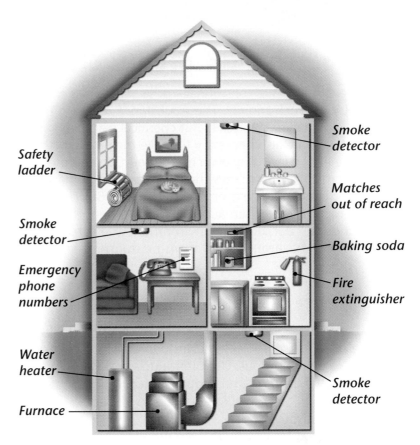

Figure 26 This fire-safe house has many of the fire-prevention features listed in Figure 25. *Interpreting Illustrations Which of those safety features can you find in the picture?*

Labels on figure: Smoke detector · Matches out of reach · Baking soda · Fire extinguisher · Smoke detector · Safety ladder · Smoke detector · Emergency phone numbers · Water heater · Furnace

Section 4 Review

1. What are the three points of the fire triangle?
2. Why is water a good tool for fighting most fires?
3. List some of the products of combustion.
4. How does adding carbon dioxide gas to cover a fire control or stop it? Use the fire triangle in your answer.
5. **Thinking Critically Making Judgments** Why is fire prevention one of the best ways to fight fires?

Science at Home

Work with your family to formulate a fire safety plan. How can fires be prevented in your home? How can fires be put out if they occur? Is there a functioning smoke detector on each floor of the home, especially near the bedrooms? How can the fire department be contacted in an emergency? Design a fire escape route. Make sure all family members know the route as well as a meeting place outside.

SCIENCE AND SOCIETY

Transporting Hazardous Chemicals

Each year, millions of tons of hazardous substances criss-cross the country by truck and rail. These substances can be poisonous, flammable, and even explosive. But chemical reactions using these materials are also necessary to make the products that people use every day. They even make the trucks themselves run.

The chemical industry says that the transport of hazardous substances is safe and that problems are rare. But public health officials are worried. When accidents do happen, these compounds can damage the environment and threaten human lives. How can hazardous substances be transported safely?

The Issues

Why Do People Transport Hazardous Substances?
Transporting hazardous substances can be dangerous. Useful products are made, however, from the hazardous materials that trucks and trains carry. Would people give up cars, computers, and CDs?

For example, CDs are made from plastics. To produce these plastics, manufacturers use compounds such as benzene and styrene. Benzene fumes are poisonous and flammable. Styrene can explode when exposed to air. Public health experts say it is important to find safe substitutes for dangerous substances. But finding alternatives will be difficult and expensive.

What Are the Risks?
Serious accidents are rare. But in the United States in a recent year, there were over 300 accidents involving hazardous chemical releases. Public health experts say that some substances are too hazardous to transport on roads and railroads. An accidental release of these substances near a city could harm many people.

Some people say that vehicles carrying chemically reactive or hazardous substances

should be restricted to isolated roads. However, many factories that use the chemical compounds are located in cities. Chemicals often must be transported from where they are made to where they are used. In the case of gasoline, cars are everywhere. Trucks and trains must transport the fuel to every neighborhood and region of the country.

How Should Transportation Be Regulated?
Manufacturers that use hazardous chemicals say that there already are adequate laws. The Hazardous Materials Transportation Act (1975, revised 1994) requires carriers of hazardous substances to follow strict labeling and packaging rules. They must keep records of what they carry and where they travel. Local emergency officials in communities near transportation routes must also be trained to handle accidents involving these substances.

On the other hand, public health experts say there are not enough inspectors to check all trucks and trains and make sure rules are followed. But hiring more inspectors would cost additional tax money.

You Decide

1. Identify the Problem
In your own words, explain the problem of safely transporting hazardous substances.

2. Analyze the Options
Examine the pros and cons of greater regulation of the transport of hazardous substances. In each position, consider the effects on chemical industries and on the general public.

3. Find a Solution
Suppose there is a chemical factory in your city. You are the emergency planning director. Create regulations for transporting hazardous substances through your community.

SECTION 1 Matter and Its Changes

Key Ideas

◆ Matter may be in the form of elements, compounds, or mixtures.

◆ Chemical changes result in the formation of new substances. Physical changes do not.

◆ Color change, production of a gas or a precipitate, a change in temperature, or a change in the properties of a substance are all clues that a chemical reaction has taken place.

◆ Chemical reactions occur when chemical bonds are formed or broken.

Key Terms

chemistry	chemical change
element	chemical reaction
compound	precipitate
mixture	atom
solution	molecule
physical change	chemical bond

SECTION 2 Describing Chemical Reactions

Key Ideas

◆ A chemical equation uses symbols to show the reactants and products of a chemical reaction.

◆ Matter is neither created nor destroyed during a chemical reaction.

◆ Chemical reactions may be classified by the types of changes in reactants and products.

Key Terms

chemical equation	conservation of mass
symbol	coefficient
chemical formula	synthesis
subscript	decomposition
reactants	replacement reaction
products	

SECTION 3 Controlling Chemical Reactions

Key Ideas

◆ Every chemical reaction involves a change in energy. Some reactions absorb energy and others release it.

◆ The rate of a chemical reaction can be controlled by such factors as concentration, surface area, temperature, and use of a catalyst or inhibitor.

Key Terms

exothermic reaction	catalyst
endothermic reaction	enzyme
activation energy	inhibitor
concentration	

SECTION 4 Fire and Fire Safety

INTEGRATING HEALTH

Key Ideas

◆ The fire triangle shows the three things necessary to start a fire and keep it burning: fuel, oxygen, and heat.

◆ Water stops combustion by keeping the fuel from coming in contact with oxygen. Also, evaporation of water uses a great deal of heat and cools the fire.

Key Terms

combustion	fuel

ACTIVITY

USING THE INTERNET

www.science-explorer.phschool.com

Reviewing Content

For more review of key concepts, see the Interactive Student Tutorial CD-ROM.

Multiple Choice

Choose the letter of the best answer.

1. A chemical equation shows
   a. elements and mixtures.
   b. hydrogen and oxygen.
   c. reactants and products.
   d. chemical bonds.
2. You can balance a chemical equation by changing the
   a. coefficients.
   b. products.
   c. reactants.
   d. formulas.
3. The reaction between sulfur trioxide and water ($SO_3 + H_2O \rightarrow H_2SO_4$) is a
   a. replacement reaction.
   b. synthesis reaction.
   c. decomposition reaction.
   d. physical change.
4. The rate of a chemical reaction can be increased by all the following, except:
   a. increasing temperature.
   b. increasing concentration.
   c. decreasing concentration.
   d. increasing surface area.
5. To extinguish a fire, do *not*
   a. remove fuel.
   b. add oxygen.
   c. reduce heat.
   d. add baking soda.

True or False

If the statement is true, write true. If it is false, change the underlined word or words to make the statement true.

6. Air, soil, and sea water are all examples of <u>elements</u>.
7. A solid that falls out of solution during a chemical reaction is called a <u>precipitate</u>.
8. A <u>chemical</u> change occurs when new substances are formed.
9. An <u>exothermic</u> reaction is a chemical reaction that absorbs heat.
10. The three parts of the fire triangle are fuel, <u>carbon dioxide</u>, and heat.

Checking Concepts

11. How can millions of compounds exist if there are only about 100 elements?
12. Why can't you balance a chemical equation by changing the subscripts?
13. You find the mass of a piece of iron metal, let it rust, and measure the mass again. The mass has increased. Does this violate the law of conservation of mass? Explain.
14. A fire starts in a frying pan in your kitchen. You grab a box of baking soda and throw its contents into the pan. Bubbling and foaming occur, and the fire goes out. What is the evidence that a chemical reaction has occurred?
15. **Writing to Learn** Imagine you are teaching a group of younger students about the difference between chemical and physical changes. One of the students claims the change from liquid water to water vapor is chemical. Write a brief paragraph of what you would say to convince the student otherwise.

Thinking Visually

16. **Concept Map** Copy the chemical reactions concept map onto a separate sheet of paper. Then complete it and add a title. (For more on concept maps, see the Skills Handbook.)

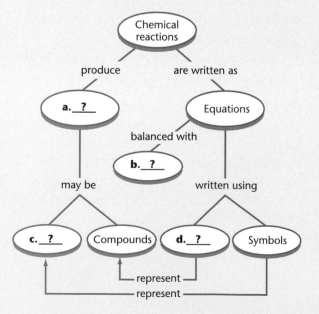

Applying Skills

Use the energy diagram to answer Questions 17–19.

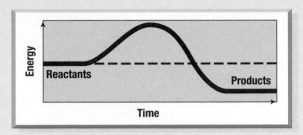

17. **Interpreting Data** How does the energy of the products compare with the energy of the reactants?
18. **Classifying** Tell whether this reaction is exothermic or endothermic.
19. **Predicting** What would happen to the graph if a catalyst were added to the reaction? Would adding heat to the reaction change the height of the curve? Explain.

Thinking Critically

20. **Applying Concepts** Balance the following equations and tell whether they are synthesis, decomposition, or replacement reactions.
    a. $Fe + HCl \rightarrow FeCl_2 + H_2$
    b. $N_2 + O_2 \rightarrow N_2O_5$
    c. $H_2CO_3 \rightarrow H_2O + CO_2$
    d. $CuO + H_2SO_4 \rightarrow CuSO_4 + H_2O$
21. **Problem Solving** Steel that is exposed to water and salt rusts quickly. If you were a shipbuilder, how would you protect a new ship? Explain why your solution works.
22. **Relating Cause and Effect** Firefighters open doors very carefully, because sometimes a room will explode into flames when the door is opened. Based on your knowledge of reaction rates and the fire triangle, why does this happen?

Performance Assessment

CHAPTER PROJECT 1 — Wrap Up

Presenting Your Project Compare the reactions in your chemical change log with those of your classmates. How many of the same processes did you observe? Defend your opinions as to whether or not your observations were chemical changes. Together make a list of the types of evidence you observed, and classify the reactions as endothermic or exothermic.

Reflect and Record In your journal, answer these questions. What evidence of chemical change is easiest to detect? What types of chemical reactions did you observe most frequently? Give an example of a chemical reaction you suspect was taking place, but for which you could not find direct evidence.

Getting Involved

In Your School With permission from your teacher, find out about the fire safety plan used in your school building. Ask administrators or custodial staff to help you check where fire safety equipment and fire alarms are located. Learn how to leave the building safely from several locations. Ask about the role of the fire department in fire drills. Make an oral report to your class or create a poster to display your findings for other classes.

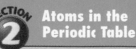

PROJECT 2

Molecule Models

With computer-made models like these, you can see molecules up close and personal. Many compounds are made of molecules—much tinier, of course, than these models.

In this chapter, you will learn why atoms react with each other. You will also learn about the different types of chemical bonds that can hold atoms together. In your project you can use fruits, vegetables, or other materials to make models of atoms and the way they bond in compounds.

Your Goal To make models showing how atoms bond in compounds that contain ionic and covalent bonds.

To complete the project you must
◆ select appropriate materials to make models of atoms
◆ design a way to tell the difference between the atoms of various elements
◆ indicate the correct number of bonds each atom forms
◆ use your model atoms to compare compounds that contain ionic and covalent bonds

Get Started Brainstorm with some of your classmates about materials you can use to make models of atoms and chemical bonds. You may want to look ahead in the chapter to preview covalent and ionic bonding.

Check Your Progress You'll be working on this project as you study this chapter. To keep your project on track, look for Check Your Progress boxes at the following points.

Section 1 Review, page 54: Make models of atoms.
Section 3 Review, page 64: Build models of ionic compounds.
Section 4 Review, page 69: Build models of compounds that contain covalent bonds.

Wrap Up At the end of the chapter (page 77), you will present and explain your models to the class.

A computer-made model of a protein shows the many atoms that are bonded together in the molecule.

SECTION 4 **Covalent Bonds**

Discover **Why Don't Water and Oil Mix?**
Sharpen Your Skills **Designing Experiments**
Skills Lab **Shedding Light on Chemical Bonds**

Integrating Earth Science

SECTION 5 **Crystal Chemistry**

Discover **How Small Do They Get?**

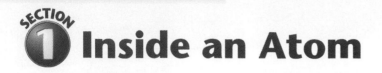
DISCOVER ·································· ACTIVITY

How Far Away Is the Electron?

1. On a piece of paper, make a small circle no bigger than a dime. The circle represents the nucleus, or center, of a model atom.

2. Measure the diameter of the circle in centimeters.

3. Now predict where you think the outer edge of this model atom will be. For example, will the outer edge be within the edges of the paper? Your desk? The classroom? The school building?

Think It Over

Making Models The diameter of an actual atom can be 100,000 times the diameter of its nucleus. Calculate the diameter of your model atom. How close was your prediction in Step 3 to your calculation? (*Hint:* To compare your result to the real world, change the units of your prediction from centimeters to meters.)

GUIDE FOR READING

◆ What is the structure of an atom?

◆ What role do valence electrons play in forming chemical bonds?

Reading Tip As you read, make a table listing the particles found in an atom. Include the name of each particle, its charge, and where in an atom the particle is located.

Picture this: It's –5°C, five degrees below the freezing temperature of water. Two white solids—ice and salt—are side by side. You begin to heat the materials to see how each one will change. As the temperature rises, the ice melts at 0°C, making liquid water. It then boils into a gas at 100°C. The water is long gone before you notice a change in the salt. Finally, at 801°C the salt begins to melt. It boils away when the temperature reaches 1,413°C.

Although these materials were both solids when you started heating them, they showed very different properties as conditions changed. These differences are caused by the kinds of chemical bonds that hold their atoms together. To understand how atoms bond, you first need to know more about atoms themselves.

Structure of an Atom

Ice, salt, and all other materials in your world are made of atoms. Atoms are so small it would take about two million to make a line across the period at the end of this sentence. It's amazing that things so tiny are the building blocks of all substances in the universe.

If you could look into a single atom, what might you see? Figuring out what atoms are made of hasn't been simple. Theories about their shape and structure have changed many times over the last 200 years and continue to change even now. But some ideas about atoms are well understood. For one thing, scientists know atoms are made of even smaller particles.

▼ Ice   Rock salt ▼

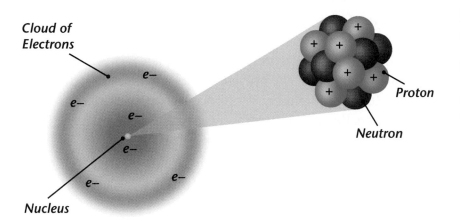

Cloud of Electrons

e–

e–

e–

e–

e–

e–

Nucleus

Proton

Neutron

Figure 1 An atom's tiny nucleus contains protons and neutrons. The electrons move in the space around the nucleus.
Applying Concepts Is this carbon atom negatively charged, positively charged, or neutral overall?

An atom consists of a nucleus surrounded by one or more electrons. The **nucleus** (NOO klee us) is the tiny, central core of an atom. It contains particles called protons and neutrons. **Protons** have a positive electric charge (indicated by a plus symbol, +). **Neutrons** have no charge. They are neutral. (Could you guess that from their name?) A third type of particles moves in the space around the nucleus. These very energetic particles, which are called **electrons,** move rapidly in all directions. Electrons carry a negative charge (indicated by a negative symbol, –).

Look at the carbon atom illustrated in Figure 1. If you count the number of protons and electrons, you'll see there are six of each. In an atom, the number of protons equals the number of electrons. As a result, the total positive charge and total negative charge balance each other, making the atom neutral. The number of neutrons in an atom may be the same as the number of protons, but not always.

Although the charges of a proton and an electron cancel each other out, the particles differ greatly in mass. A proton is almost 2,000 times as massive as an electron! Neutrons, however, have about the same mass as protons.

Figure 2 A window fan is a model for the way electrons fill the space around the nucleus of an atom.

✓ *Checkpoint* Which particles in an atom are in the nucleus?

Electrons in Atoms

Electrons move around the nucleus so rapidly that it is impossible to know exactly where any electron is at a particular time. Think about a window fan blowing air. The fan blades move too fast for you to see them. You know there are gaps between the blades, but where are the blades? As electrons move around the nucleus, the effect is like the fan blades, but in three dimensions. You can think of the space around the nucleus as a spherical cloud of negatively charged electrons.

Little Particles, Big Spaces Most of the mass of an atom comes from its protons and neutrons. But the atom's volume is the space in which the electrons move. This space is huge compared to the space occupied by the nucleus. To picture the difference, imagine standing at the pitcher's mound in a baseball stadium. If the nucleus were the size of a pencil eraser, the electrons could be in the outfield or as far away as the top row of seats!

☑ *Checkpoint* *Where are the electrons in an atom?*

Models of Atoms

For over two centuries, models of atoms have helped scientists understand why matter behaves as it does. As scientists have learned more, the model of the atom has changed.

1808
Dalton Model

British chemist John Dalton published his *New System of Chemical Philosophy*, explaining that each element is made of small atoms and that different elements have atoms of different mass. Dalton imagined atoms as tiny, solid balls.

1897
Thomson Model

British scientist, J. J. Thomson, proposed a new model. He suggested that an atom is a positively-charged sphere with electrons embedded in it. His model could be described as looking like a muffin with berries scattered through it.

1800

1900

For almost 100 years, not much ▲ new information was learned about atoms.

5+

1904 Nagaoka Model

Japanese physicist Hantaro Nagaoka proposed a model of the atom that had a large sphere in the center with a positive charge. His model showed the electrons revolving around this sphere like the planets around the sun.

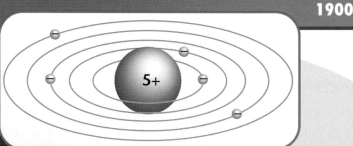

Valence Electrons The electrons in an atom aren't all the same distance away from the nucleus. The electrons farthest from the nucleus are called **valence electrons** (VAY luns). Only valence electrons are involved in bonding. The number of valence electrons is the key to whether or not an atom bonds with another atom. You could say the number of valence electrons is the "face" an atom shows to other atoms. Just as you react to expressions on other people's faces, atoms react with each other as a result of how many valence electrons each has.

In Your Journal

Find out more about one of the scientists who worked on models of the atom. Write an imaginary interview with this person in which you discuss his work with him.

1911
Rutherford Model

British physicist Ernest Rutherford concluded that the atom is mostly empty space. Electrons orbit randomly around a small, positively charged nucleus.

1932
Chadwick Model

British physicist James Chadwick discovered the neutron, a particle having about the same mass as the proton but with no electrical charge. The existence of the neutron explained why atoms were heavier than the total mass of their protons and electrons.

1910   1920   1930   1940   1950

1913
Bohr Model

Danish physicist Niels Bohr determined that electrons aren't randomly located around the nucleus. His model showed electrons moving in specific layers, or shells. He said that atoms absorb or give off energy when the electrons move from one shell to another.

Cloud of electrons

1920s to Present
Modern Model

The current model of the atom came from the work of many scientists from the 1920s to the present. It shows the electrons as forming a negatively charged cloud around the nucleus. It is impossible to determine exactly where an electron is at any given time.

Figure 3 In electron dot diagrams, each dot represents one outer, or valence, electron of an atom. *Interpreting Diagrams* Each hydrogen atom has only one electron, but an argon atom has 18 electrons. How many of argon's electrons are valence electrons?

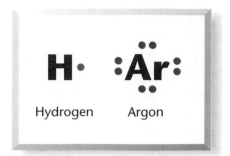

Hydrogen   Argon

One way to show the number of valence electrons is with an **electron dot diagram.** It includes the symbol for an element surrounded by dots. Each dot stands for one valence electron.

Why Atoms Form Bonds

A neutral atom never has more than eight valence electrons. Most kinds of atoms have fewer. When atoms form bonds with each other, one of two things usually happens. Either the number of valence electrons increases to a total of eight, or all the valence electrons are lost. When atoms end up with eight or zero valence electrons, they become less reactive than they were before. Chemists say that such atoms are more chemically stable.

A chemical bond forms between two atoms when valence electrons move between them. Electrons may be transferred from one atom to another, or they may be shared between the atoms. In either case, the change causes the atoms to become connected, or bonded. Chemical reactions occur when bonds between atoms form. Reactions also occur when bonds are broken. Each time, electrons are moved around. The result is the formation of new substances.

Section 1 Review

1. Describe the parts of an atom and tell where each is found.
2. Explain why the electrical charge on an atom is zero, or neutral.
3. What happens to valence electrons during the formation of chemical bonds?
4. Explain why electrons make up much of an atom's volume but not much of its mass.
5. **Thinking Critically Applying Concepts** What information can you get from an electron dot diagram?

Check Your Progress
CHAPTER PROJECT 2
Select materials to use to build your models. Start by making models of several common elements such as hydrogen, oxygen, nitrogen, carbon, chlorine, sodium, potassium, and sulfur. (*Hint:* You will need to represent the valence electrons on each atom.) Make several atoms of each element and save them. Select materials to represent the chemical bonds.

SECTION
2 Atoms in the Periodic Table

DISCOVER · ACTIVITY

What Are the Trends in the Periodic Table?

1. Examine closely the periodic table of the elements your teacher provides. Each square shows the chemical symbol for an element plus information about the element.
2. Look in each square for the whole number located above the symbol of the element. As you read across a row from left to right, what trend do you see?
3. Now look at a column from top to bottom. What pattern do you see in these numbers?

Think It Over

Interpreting Data Are the elements organized in alphabetical order? Can you explain why one row ends and a new row starts? Why do you think certain elements are in the same column? What questions would you need to ask in order to understand how the elements are organized?

Mix some elements together and nothing happens. Mix other elements together and they react as explosively as the sodium and bromine in Figure 4. Other combinations of elements react either slowly or only when heated. Recall that atoms react with each other as a result of how many valence electrons each has. Therefore, knowing the number of valence electrons in atoms is a clue to which elements combine, and how. But where do you look for this information? You can look in the periodic table of the elements.

GUIDE FOR READING

◆ How is the periodic table organized?

◆ What do elements in a family have in common?

Reading Tip As you read, use the periodic table in Appendix D for reference. Look for repeating patterns.

Organizing the Elements

The periodic table is a system used worldwide for organizing elements into categories based on how they react. The way the elements are organized in the periodic table also tells you something about their protons and electrons.

All the atoms of one kind of element have the same number of protons. For example, all carbon atoms have six protons, and all hydrogen atoms have only one. The **atomic number** is the number of protons in the nucleus of an atom. **Look at any periodic table and you will see that elements are arranged from left to right and top to bottom in order of increasing atomic number.** Remember that if you know the number of protons in an atom, you also know the number of electrons.

Figure 4 The elements sodium and bromine react with an explosion.

Periodic Table of the Elements

1																	18
1 1 **H**	2											13	14	15	16	17	2 **He**
2 3 **Li**	4 **Be**											5 **B**	6 **C**	7 **N**	8 **O**	9 **F**	10 **Ne**
3 11 **Na**	12 **Mg**	3	4	5	6	7	8	9	10	11	12	13 **Al**	14 **Si**	15 **P**	16 **S**	17 **Cl**	18 **Ar**
4 19 **K**	20 **Ca**	21 **Sc**	22 **Ti**	23 **V**	24 **Cr**	25 **Mn**	26 **Fe**	27 **Co**	28 **Ni**	29 **Cu**	30 **Zn**	31 **Ga**	32 **Ge**	33 **As**	34 **Se**	35 **Br**	36 **Kr**
5 37 **Rb**	38 **Sr**	39 **Y**	40 **Zr**	41 **Nb**	42 **Mo**	43 **Tc**	44 **Ru**	45 **Rh**	46 **Pd**	47 **Ag**	48 **Cd**	49 **In**	50 **Sn**	51 **Sb**	52 **Te**	53 **I**	54 **Xe**
6 55 **Cs**	56 **Ba**	57 **La**	72 **Hf**	73 **Ta**	74 **W**	75 **Re**	76 **Os**	77 **Ir**	78 **Pt**	79 **Au**	80 **Hg**	81 **Tl**	82 **Pb**	83 **Bi**	84 **Po**	85 **At**	86 **Rn**
7 87 **Fr**	88 **Ra**	89 **Ac**	104 **Rf**	105 **Db**	106 **Sg**	107 **Bh**	108 **Hs**	109 **Mt**	110 **Uun**	111 **Uuu**	112 **Uub**						

58 **Ce**	59 **Pr**	60 **Nd**	61 **Pm**	62 **Sm**	63 **Eu**	64 **Gd**	65 **Tb**	66 **Dy**	67 **Ho**	68 **Er**	69 **Tm**	70 **Yb**	71 **Lu**
90 **Th**	91 **Pa**	92 **U**	93 **Np**	94 **Pu**	95 **Am**	96 **Cm**	97 **Bk**	98 **Cf**	99 **Es**	100 **Fm**	101 **Md**	102 **No**	103 **Lr**

Figure 5 The periodic table organizes the elements into rows and columns.

Sharpen your Skills

Classifying

ACTIVITY

Match each element on the left with the element on the right that has the most similar chemical properties. Use the periodic table to help you.

Krypton (Kr)	Sodium (Na)
Phosphorus (P)	Neon (Ne)
Potassium (K)	Calcium (Ca)
Magnesium (Mg)	Sulfur (S)
Silicon (Si)	Nitrogen (N)
Oxygen (O)	Carbon (C)

Why did you match the pairs as you did?

Elements in the same column, up and down, are called a **group,** or **family.** Notice the numbers 1 through 18 across the tops of the columns in Figure 5. These numbers identify the group to which an element belongs. For example, carbon (C) is in Group 14 and oxygen (O) is in Group 16.

A row across the table is called a **period.** Hydrogen and helium make up the first period. The second period starts with lithium (Li) and continues across to neon (Ne). Notice that the atomic number increases one at a time from left to right across the periodic table. The number of valence electrons increases from left to right, too. Figure 6 shows the electron dot diagrams for the elements in the second period of the table.

☑ *Checkpoint* *What is the difference betweeen a group and a period in the periodic table?*

Comparing Families of Elements

If you saw a flock of ducks on a pond, would you notice any similarities among the birds? Would they share characteristics that would set them apart from crows or robins on the nearby shore? **Each family in the periodic table has its own characteristic properties based on its number of valence electrons.**

Noble Gases Group 18 at the far right side of the table is a good place to start learning about the characteristics of the families. Except for helium, atoms of these elements have eight valence electrons. (Look at the electron dot diagram for neon at right, as an example.) The Group 18 elements are known as the noble gases or inert gases. *Inert* means "inactive." Since they already have the maximum number of valence electrons, noble gas atoms don't react very easily with other atoms. Helium, which is as unreactive as the other noble gases, is stable with only two valence electrons.

Reactive Nonmetals Now look at the column to the left of the noble gases. The elements in Group 17, also called the **halogen** family, are very reactive. Atoms of these elements have seven valence electrons, as illustrated by flourine in Figure 6. A gain of just one electron leads to the more stable number of eight. As a result, elements in the halogen family react easily with other elements whose atoms can give up electrons.

Reactive Metals At the far left side of the periodic table is Group 1, the elements of the alkali metal family. If alkali metals lose one electron, the atoms are left with zero valence electrons. They become more chemically stable. This property makes the alkali metals very reactive elements. If the alkali metals lose electrons easily and the halogens gain electrons easily, what happens when they come in contact with each other? They react violently! This explains the explosive reaction between sodium and bromine shown at the beginning of this section. These two elements form the compound sodium bromide.

Hydrogen is located above Group 1 on the periodic table because it has only one valence electron. Like the alkali metal elements, hydrogen is extremely reactive.

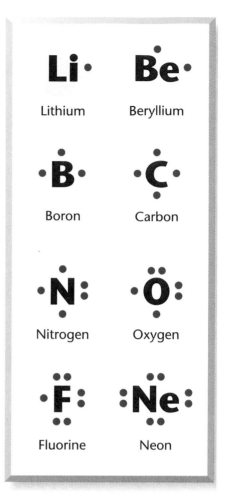

Figure 6 These eight elements make up the second period. *Calculating What is the trend in number of valence electrons from lithium to neon?*

Section 2 Review

1. What is the basis for arranging the elements in the periodic table?
2. Why are the elements in each group in the periodic table considered a family?
3. What properties are shared by the noble gases?
4. **Thinking Critically Applying Concepts** How can you use the arrangement of elements in the periodic table to predict how they will react with other elements to form compounds?

Science at Home

People use many organization systems. Think of tools in a workshop or baseball cards in a collection. Look around your home for as many different systems of organization you can find. Check out drawers and cabinets. Look for things lined up in rows. Then discuss with your family how these systems of organization compare with the periodic table of the elements.

Comparing Atom Sizes

In this lab, you will be using models to compare the sizes of atoms in one family of elements in the periodic table.

Problem

How is the radius of an atom related to its atomic number?

Materials

drawing compass
calculator
periodic table of the elements (Appendix D)

Procedure ✂

1. Using the periodic table as a reference, predict whether the size (radius) of atoms will increase, remain the same, or decrease as you go from the top to the bottom of a chemical family.

2. Look at the table on this page that lists each element in Group 2 and its atomic radius.

3. Calculate the relative radius of each atom compared to beryllium, the smallest atom listed. Do this by dividing each radius in the table by the value for beryllium. (*Hint:* The relative radius of magnesium would be 160 divided by 112, or 1.4.) Copy the table and record these values, rounded to the nearest tenth.

4. Using a compass, draw a circle for each element with a radius that corresponds to the relative radius you calculated in Step 3. Use centimeters as your unit for the radius of each of these circles. **CAUTION:** *Do not push the sharp point of the compass against your skin.*

5. Label each model with the symbol of the element it represents.

DATA TABLE

Atomic Number	Element	Radius (pm)*	Relative Radius
4	Be	112	1
12	Mg	160	
20	Ca	197	
38	Sr	215	
56	Ba	222	

*A picometer (pm) is one billionth of a millimeter.

Analyze and Conclude

1. Based on your models, was your prediction in Step 1 correct? Explain your answer.

2. Make a graph of the data given in the first and third columns of your table. Label the horizontal axis Atomic Number. Mark the divisions from 0 to 60. Then label the vertical axis Radius and mark its divisions from 0 to 300 picometers.

3. Do your points fall on a straight line or on a curve? What pattern does your graph show?

4. Predict where you would find the largest atom in any chemical family. What evidence would you need to tell if your prediction is correct?

5. **Think About It** If an atom has an actual radius of 100 to 200 picometers, why would drawing a model with a radius of about one to two centimeters be useful?

More to Explore

Look up the atomic masses for the Group 2 elements. Devise a plan to model their relative atomic masses using real-world objects.

SECTION
3 Ionic Bonds

DISCOVER · ACTIVITY · · · ·

How Do Ions Form?

1. Place three pairs of checkers (three red and three black) on your desk. The red represent electrons and the black represent protons.

2. Place nine pairs of checkers (nine red and nine black) in a separate group on your desk.

3. Move a red checker from the smaller group to the larger group.

4. Count the number of positive charges (protons) and negative charges (electrons) in each group.

5. Now sort the checkers into a group of four pairs and a group of eight pairs. Repeat Steps 3 and 4, this time moving two red checkers from the smaller group to the larger group.

Think It Over

Forming Operational Definitions What is the total charge on each group before you moved the red checkers (electrons)? What is the charge on each group after you moved the checkers? Based on this activity, what do you think happens to the charge of an atom when it loses electrons? When it gains electrons?

Imagine you are walking down the street with your best friend. A market has a bin of apples for sale. A sign says that they cost 40 cents each. You both want an apple, but your friend has only 35 cents while you have 45 cents. What can you do? It doesn't take you long to figure out that if you give your friend a nickel, you can each buy an apple. Transferring the nickel to your friend gets both of you what you want. Your actions model, in a simple way, what can happen between atoms.

Electron Transfer

Like your friend with not quite enough money to buy an apple, an atom with five, six, or seven valence electrons has not quite enough to total the more stable number of eight. On the other hand, an atom with one, two, or three valence electrons has a few it can lose. When atoms have fewer than four valence electrons, they can transfer these to other atoms that have more than four. In this way, atoms either gain electrons or lose electrons, becoming more stable.

GUIDE FOR READING

◆ How does an atom become an ion?

◆ What are the characteristic properties of ionic compounds?

◆ How are the ions in an ionic compound held together?

Reading Tip As you read, make an outline describing the characteristics of compounds containing ionic bonds.

Figure 7 When an atom loses one of its negatively charged electrons, it becomes a positively charged ion.

Two atoms talking together...

I just lost an electron!

Are you sure?

I'm positive!

Figure 8 Positively charged ions have lost one or more electrons. Negatively charged ions have gained one or more electrons. *Classifying Which ions in the table are positively charged and which are negatively charged?*

Ions and Their Charges		
Name	**Charge**	**Symbol or Formula**
Lithium	1+	Li^+
Sodium	1+	Na^+
Potassium	1+	K^+
Ammonium	1+	NH_4^+
Calcium	2+	Ca^{2+}
Magnesium	2+	Mg^{2+}
Aluminum	3+	Al^{3+}
Fluoride	1–	F^-
Chloride	1–	Cl^-
Iodide	1–	I^-
Bicarbonate	1–	HCO_3^-
Nitrate	1–	NO_3^-
Oxide	2–	O^{2-}
Sulfide	2–	S^{2-}
Carbonate	2–	CO_3^{2-}
Sulfate	2–	SO_4^{2-}
Phosphate	3–	PO_4^{3-}

An **ion** (EYE ahn) is an atom or group of atoms that has become electrically charged. **When an atom loses an electron, it loses a negative charge and becomes a positive ion. When an atom gains an electron, it gains a negative charge and becomes a negative ion.**

Forming an Ionic Bond

Follow what happens to sodium and chlorine atoms in *Exploring Ionic Bonds.* Note how many valence electrons each atom has. The transfer of sodium's one valence electron to chlorine changes both atoms into ions. The sodium atom becomes a positive ion (Na^+). The chlorine atom becomes a negative ion (Cl^-). Negative and positive electric charges attract each other, so the oppositely charged Na^+ and Cl^- ions come together. They form sodium chloride, which you know as table salt.

An **ionic bond** is the attraction between two oppositely charged ions. This attraction is similar to the attraction between opposite poles of a magnet. When the two ions come together, the opposite charges cancel out. Every sodium ion (with a charge written as 1+) is balanced by a chloride ion (with a charge written as 1–). The formula for sodium chloride, NaCl, shows you this 1 : 1 ratio.

Compounds are electrically neutral. When ions come together, they do so in a way that balances out the charges on the ions. Figure 8 lists some common ions. Look at the charge of the magnesium ion. How many chloride ions would be needed to cancel out the 2+ charge of magnesium in the compound magnesium chloride? The formula for magnesium chloride, $MgCl_2$, tells you the answer is two.

☑ *Checkpoint* *What effect does gaining an electron have on the charge of an atom?*

EXPLORING Ionic Bonds

Reactions between metals and nonmetals often form ionic compounds. These reactions occur easily between the metals in Group 1 and the halogens in Group 17. Here you can see what happens when an ionic bond forms between sodium and chlorine.

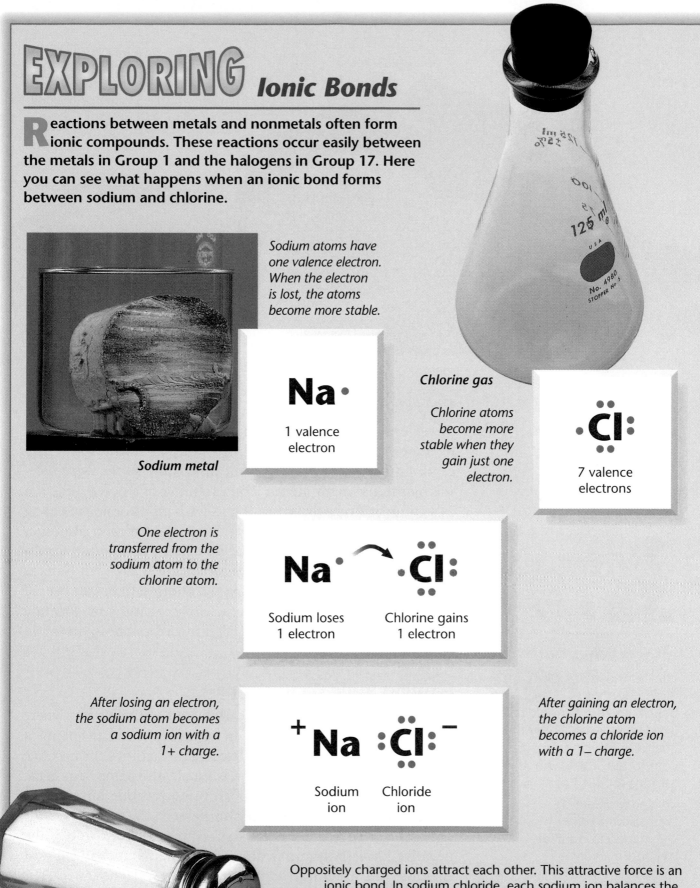

Sodium atoms have one valence electron. When the electron is lost, the atoms become more stable.

Na·

1 valence electron

Sodium metal

Chlorine gas

Chlorine atoms become more stable when they gain just one electron.

·Cl:

7 valence electrons

One electron is transferred from the sodium atom to the chlorine atom.

Na· ⤳ **·Cl:**

Sodium loses 1 electron   Chlorine gains 1 electron

After losing an electron, the sodium atom becomes a sodium ion with a 1+ charge.

⁺Na :Cl:⁻

Sodium ion   Chloride ion

After gaining an electron, the chlorine atom becomes a chloride ion with a 1– charge.

Oppositely charged ions attract each other. This attractive force is an ionic bond. In sodium chloride, each sodium ion balances the charge of one chloride ion. Overall, the compound sodium chloride is electrically neutral.

Sodium chloride

Figure 9 What do seashells, chalk, limestone, and eggshells have in common? They all contain calcium carbonate, which is an ionic compound made of Ca^{2+} and CO_3^{2-} ions.

Polyatomic Ions

Some ions are made of more than one atom. Ions that are made of more than one atom are examples of **polyatomic ions** (pahl ee uh TAHM ik). The prefix *poly* means "many," so the word *poly- atomic* means "many atoms." You can think of a polyatomic ion as a group of atoms that react as one. Each polyatomic ion has an overall positive or negative charge. If a polyatomic ion combines with another ion of opposite charge, an ionic compound forms. Think, for example, about the carbonate ion (CO_3^{2-}). It is made of one carbon atom and three oxygen atoms and has an overall charge of 2–. This ion can combine with a calcium ion, forming calcium carbonate ($CaCO_3$). Calcium carbonate is the main compound in limestone.

Naming Ionic Compounds

Magnesium chloride, sodium bicarbonate, sodium oxide—where do these names come from? For an ionic compound, the name of the positive ion comes first, followed by the name of the negative ion. The name of the positive ion is usually the name of a metal. It may also be the name of a positive polyatomic ion, such as ammonium. If the negative ion is an element, the end of its name changes to *-ide*. For example, MgO is magnesium oxide. If the negative ion is polyatomic, its name remains unchanged. For example, the chemical name for baking soda ($NaHCO_3$) is sodium carbonate.

✓ *Checkpoint* What kind of atom has a name change when it becomes an ion?

Properties of Ionic Compounds

Do you think salt, iron rust, baking soda, and limestone are very much alike? If you answer no, you're right. If you answer yes, you're right, too! You wouldn't want to season your food with rust, or construct a building out of baking soda. But despite their differences, these compounds share some similarities because they all contain ionic bonds. **The characteristic properties of ionic compounds include crystal shape, high melting points, and electrical conductivity.**

Crystal Shape The object in Figure 10 that looks like a glass sculpture is really a chunk of halite, or table salt. Halite is an ionic compound. All samples of halite show these sharp edges, corners, and flat surfaces. The shapes result from how the ions are arranged. In solid sodium chloride, the Na^+ and Cl^- ions come together in an alternating pattern, as shown in the diagram. The ions form an orderly, three-dimensional arrangement called a **crystal.**

In an ionic compound, every ion is attracted to ions near it that have an opposite charge. Positive ions tend to be near negative ions and farther from other positive ions. As a result, a positive sodium ion doesn't bond with just one negative chloride ion. It bonds with ions above, below and to all sides. The chloride ions do the same with sodium ions, so a crystal forms. This pattern continues no matter what the size of the crystal. In a single grain of salt, the crystal can extend for millions of ions in every direction. The number of sodium ions and chloride ions in the crystal is equal. The formula for sodium chloride, NaCl, represents this 1 : 1 ratio.

Crystal Clear

Can you grow a salt crystal?

1. Add salt to a jar containing about 200 mL of hot tap water, and stir. Keep adding salt until no more dissolves and it settles out when you stop stirring.

2. Tie a large crystal of coarse salt into the middle of a piece of thread.

3. Tie one end of the thread to the middle of a pencil.

4. Suspend the other end of the thread in the solution by laying the pencil across the mouth of the jar. Do not allow the crystal to touch the solution.

5. Place the jar in a quiet, undisturbed area. Check the size of the crystal over the next few days.

Observing Does the salt crystal change size over time? What is its shape? What do you think is happening to the salt in the solution?

Na^+

Cl^-

Figure 10 A halite crystal contains sodium and chloride ions in an alternating pattern.
Making Generalizations What general characteristics of crystals can you observe in the photograph of halite?

Figure 11 A conductivity tester shows that a solution of salt in water conducts electricity. The bulb lights up because the ions in the salt solution complete the circuit for the flow of electricity.

High Melting Points What happens when you heat an ionic compound such as table salt? Remember, the ions are held together in a crystal by attractions between oppositely charged particles. When the particles have enough energy to overcome the attractive forces between them, they break away from each other. It takes a temperature of 801°C to reach this energy for table salt. Ionic bonds are strong enough to cause all ionic compounds to be solids at room temperature.

Electrical Conductivity When ionic compounds dis-

INTEGRATING PHYSICS solve in water, the solution conducts electricity. Electricity is the flow of electric charge, and ions have electric charges. However, if you connect wires from a salt crystal to a battery and a light bulb, don't expect anything to happen. A solid ionic compound does not conduct electricity very well. The ions in the crystal are tightly bound to each other. If the charged particles do not move, electricity does not flow. But what if the ions are broken apart? When ionic compounds dissolve in water, the ions separate. These ions then move freely, and the solution conducts electricity.

Melting ionic compounds also allows them to conduct electricity. Can you figure out why? Think about the difference between the particles in a solid and a liquid. In a solid, the particles do not move from place to place. But in a liquid, the particles slip and slide past each other. As long as the ions can move around, electricity can flow.

Section 3 Review

1. How does an ion form from an atom?
2. What properties may be used to identify ionic compounds?
3. Why are ions in an ionic compound attracted to each other?
4. Name these compounds: NaF, BeI_2, K_2SO_4, CaO, H_2S, $MgCO_3$.
5. Solid salt does not conduct electricity. How then does dissolving salt in water allow electricity to flow?
6. **Thinking Critically Problem Solving** The metal scandium (Sc) has three valence electrons. What is the formula of the ionic compound formed when scandium reacts with iodine?

Check Your Progress

CHAPTER PROJECT 2

Use your model atoms to make models of compounds containing ionic bonds, such as sodium chloride (NaCl), magnesium chloride ($MgCl_2$), or potassium oxide (K_2O). (*Hint:* Figure out whether each atom forms a positive or negative ion. Then use combinations that result in a neutral compound.)

SECTION 4 Covalent Bonds

DISCOVER ·· ACTIVITY ···

Why Don't Water and Oil Mix?

1. Fill a small jar that has a tight-fitting top about a third full with water.

2. Add an equal amount of vegetable oil to the water and cover the jar tightly.

3. Shake the jar vigorously for approximately 15–20 seconds. Observe.

4. Allow the jar to sit undisturbed for about 1 minute. Observe again.

5. Remove the top and add 2–3 drops of liquid soap. Repeat Steps 3 and 4.

Think It Over

Inferring Describe how adding soap affected the mixing of the oil and water. How might your observations depend on chemical bonds in the soap, oil, and water molecules?

Remember the market with apples selling for 40 cents each? On another day, the apples are also on sale at two for 70 cents. You and your friend check your pockets and find 35 cents each. What can you do? You could give your friend a nickel to make enough money for one apple. Then you would have only 30 cents, not enough to get one for yourself. But if you share your money, together you can buy two apples.

Electron Sharing

Just as you and your friend can buy apples by sharing money, atoms can become more stable by sharing valence electrons. A chemical bond formed when two atoms share electrons is called a **covalent bond.**

Unlike ionic bonds, which form between metals and nonmetals, covalent bonds often form between two or more nonmetals. Oxygen, carbon, nitrogen, and the halogens are examples of atoms that frequently bond to other nonmetals by sharing electrons.

The element fluorine forms molecules made of two fluorine atoms. Each fluorine atom shares one of its seven valence electrons with the other atom. When you count the number of electrons on one atom, you count the shared pair each time. By sharing, both atoms have eight valence electrons. **In a covalent bond, both atoms attract the two shared electrons at the same time.**

GUIDE FOR READING

◆ What happens to electrons in a covalent bond?

◆ Why do some atoms in covalent bonds have slight negative or positive charges?

◆ Why are polar and nonpolar compounds different?

Reading Tip Before you read, preview the illustrations in the section. Predict how covalent bonds differ from ionic bonds.

Figure 12 The shared pair of electrons in a molecule of fluorine is a single covalent bond.

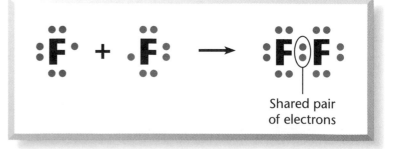

Shared pair of electrons

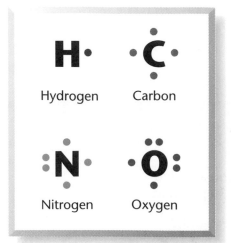

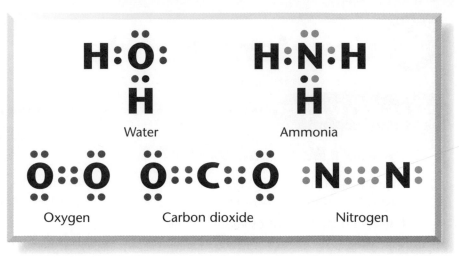

Figure 13 The electron dot diagrams for hydrogen, carbon, nitrogen, and oxygen (left) show the number of valence electrons for each. The diagrams of molecules (right) show how the electrons are shared in covalent bonds. *Interpreting Diagrams How many bonds does each nitrogen atom form?*

How Many Bonds?

Look at the electron dot diagrams for oxygen, nitrogen, and carbon atoms in Figure 13. Count the dots on each atom. The number of bonds these atoms can form equals the number of valence electrons needed to make a total of eight.

For example, oxygen has six valence electrons, so it can form two covalent bonds. In a water molecule, oxygen forms one covalent bond with each hydrogen atom. Since nitrogen has five valence electrons, it can form three bonds. In ammonia (NH_3), a nitrogen atom bonds with three hydrogen atoms.

Next, compare water to a molecule of oxygen. Can you find the two covalent bonds? This time *two* pairs of electrons are shared between the oxygen atoms, forming a **double bond.** In a carbon dioxide molecule, carbon forms two double bonds—each with two different oxygen atoms. In some compounds, nitrogen and carbon atoms can even form triple bonds.

Count the electrons around any atom in the compounds in Figure 13. Remember that shared pairs count for both atoms forming a bond. You'll find that each atom has eight valence electrons. The exception is hydrogen, which can have no more than two electrons and forms one bond.

Properties of Molecular Compounds

Molecular compounds consist of molecules having covalently bonded atoms. Such compounds have very different properties from ionic compounds.

Look at Figure 14, which lists the melting and boiling points for some molecular compounds. Quite a difference

Figure 14 Molecular compounds have much lower melting points than ionic compounds.

Melting and Boiling Points of Some Molecular Compounds			
Compound	Formula	Melting Point (°C)	Boiling Point (°C)
Water	H_2O	0	100
Methane	CH_4	–182	–164
Carbon dioxide	CO_2	—	–78.6*
Ammonia	NH_3	–77.7	–33.6
Rubbing alcohol	C_3H_8O	–89.5	82.4
Sugar	$C_{12}H_{22}O_{11}$	185–186	(decomposes)

*Carbon dioxide changes directly from a solid to a gas.

from the 801°C and 1,413°C described earlier for salt! In molecular solids, the molecules are held close to each other. But the forces holding them are much weaker than those holding ions together in an ionic solid. Less heat is needed to separate molecules than is needed to separate ions. Some molecular compounds, such as sugar and water (ice), do form crystals. But these, like other molecular solids, melt and boil at much lower temperatures than ionic compounds do.

Most molecular compounds are poor conductors of electricity. No charged particles are available to move, and electricity does not flow. That's why molecular compounds, such as plastic and rubber, are used to insulate electric wires. Even as liquids, molecular compounds are poor conductors. Pure water, for example, does not conduct electricity. Neither does water with sugar dissolved in it.

☑ *Checkpoint* Why are molecular compounds poor conductors?

Unequal Sharing of Electrons

Have you ever played tug of war? If you have, you know that if both teams have equal strength, the contest is a tie. But what if the teams pull on the rope with unequal force? Then the rope moves closer to one side or the other. The same is true of electrons in a covalent bond. **Some atoms pull more strongly on the shared electrons than other atoms do. As a result, the electrons move closer to one atom, causing the atoms to have slight electrical charges.** These charges are not as strong as the charges on ions. But the unequal sharing is enough to make one atom slightly negative and the other atom slightly positive. A covalent bond in which electrons are shared unequally is **polar.**

Sharpen your Skills

Designing Experiments

Suppose you have samples  **ACTIVITY** of two colorless, odorless gases. You are told that one gas is methane (CH_4) and the other is carbon dioxide (CO_2). How could you use the information in Figure 14 to find out which gas is which? Describe the experiment you would set up. Tell what conditions you would control and what you would change. What result would you look for to get an answer?

Figure 15 The unequal sharing of the electrons in a polar covalent bond is like a tug of war in which one atom is slightly stronger than the other atom.

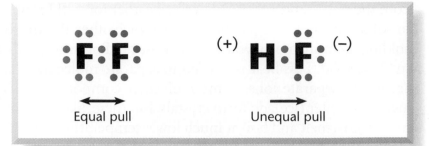

Figure 16 In the nonpolar bond in F_2, the two flourine atoms pull equally on the shared electrons. In the polar bond in HF, fluorine pulls more strongly on the shared electrons than hydrogen does.

Equal pull

Unequal pull

If two atoms pull equally on the electrons, neither atom becomes charged. This is the case when the two atoms are identical, as in fluorine gas (F_2). The valence electrons are shared equally and the bond is **nonpolar.** Compare the bond in F_2 with the polar bond in hydrogen fluoride (HF) in Figure 16.

Nonpolar Molecules Keep tug of war in mind as you look at the carbon dioxide (CO_2) molecule in Figure 17. Oxygen attracts electrons much more strongly than carbon, so bonds between oxygen and carbon are polar. But the two oxygen atoms are pulling with equal strength in opposite directions. In a sense, they cancel each other out. Overall, a carbon dioxide molecule is nonpolar even though it has polar bonds. A molecule is nonpolar if it contains polar bonds that cancel each other. As you might guess, molecules that contain only nonpolar bonds are also nonpolar.

Polar Molecules Water molecules are polar. As you can see in Figure 17, the shape of the molecule leaves the two hydrogen atoms more to one end and the oxygen atom toward the other. The oxygen atom pulls electrons closer to it from both hydrogen atoms. Overall, the molecule is polar. It has a slightly negative charge at the oxygen end and a slightly positive charge near the hydrogen atoms.

✓ *Checkpoint* *What makes a covalent bond polar?*

Attractions Between Molecules

If you could shrink small enough to move among a bunch of water molecules, what would you find? The negatively charged oxygen ends and positively charged hydrogen ends behave like poles of a bar magnet. They attract the opposite ends of other water molecules. These attractions between positive and negative ends pull water molecules toward each other.

What about carbon dioxide? There is no pulling between these molecules. Remember, carbon dioxide molecules are nonpolar. No oppositely charged ends means there are no strong attractions between the molecules.

Language Arts
CONNECTION

Breaking a word into its parts can help you understand its meaning. Take *covalent,* for example. The prefix *co-* means "together." The *-valent* part comes from "valence electrons." So "valence electrons together" can remind you that in a covalent bond, valence electrons are shared.

In Your Journal

The prefix *co-* is used in many other words—*coauthor, coexist,* and *cooperate* are just a few. Add five more *co-* words to this list and try to define them all without looking them up. Then check their meanings in a dictionary and write sentences that use each one.

CO₂ molecule (nonpolar)

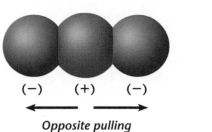

(−)   (+)   (−)

Opposite pulling
cancels

H₂O molecule (polar)

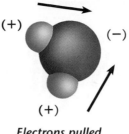

(+)   (−)

(+)

Electrons pulled
towards oxygen

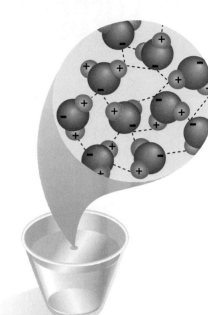

Figure 17 CO_2 molecules are nonpolar, and H_2O molecules are polar. Attractions between the slightly positive and slightly negative ends of water molecules pull the molecules toward each other (below).

   Differences in the attractions between molecules lead to different properties in polar and nonpolar compounds. For example, water and vegetable oil don't mix. Oil is nonpolar, and nonpolar compounds do not dissolve well in water. The polar water molecules are attracted more strongly to each other than to the molecules of oil. Water stays with water and oil stays with oil.

INTEGRATING TECHNOLOGY These differences in attractions come in handy when you wash laundry. Many kinds of dirt—for example, grease—are nonpolar compounds. Their molecules won't mix with plain water. So how can you wash dirt out of your clothes?

   As you found if you did the Discover activity, adding soap helped the oil and water to mix. When you do laundry, detergent causes the nonpolar dirt to mix with the polar water. Soaps and detergents have long molecules. One end of a soap molecule is polar, and the other end is nonpolar. Soaps and detergents dissolve in water because the polar ends of their molecules are attracted to water molecules. Meanwhile, their nonpolar ends mix easily with the dirt. When the water washes down the drain, the soap and the dirt go with it.

Section 4 Review

1. How are valence electrons involved in the formation of a covalent bond?
2. How do atoms in covalent bonds become slightly negative or slightly positive?
3. Explain how attractions between molecules could cause water to have a higher boiling point than carbon dioxide.
4. **Thinking Critically Comparing and Contrasting** In terms of electrons, how is a covalent bond different from an ionic bond?

Check Your Progress
CHAPTER PROJECT 2
Use your models to build simple molecules having single covalent bonds. Also make models of compounds containing double or triple bonds. (*Hint:* After you make bonds, each atom should have a total of eight valence electrons or, in the case of hydrogen, two valence electrons.)

SHEDDING LIGHT ON CHEMICAL BONDS

Electricity is the flow of electric current. In this lab, you will interpret data about which compounds conduct electricity in order to determine the nature of their bonds.

Problem

How can you use a conductivity tester to determine whether a compound contains ionic or covalent bonds?

Materials

2 1.5-V dry cells
small beaker
plastic spoon
sodium chloride
small light bulb and socket
4 lengths of wire for connections with insulation
    scraped off ends
100-mL graduated cylinder
additional substances supplied by your teacher

DATA TABLE	
Sample	Observations
Water	
Sodium chloride in water	

Procedure

1. Make a conductivity tester by following the instructions below. After you have constructed it, make a data table in your notebook similar to the one above.

2. Pour about 50 mL of water into a small beaker. Place the free ends of the two wires of the conductivity tester into the water. Be sure the ends are close but not touching each other. Record your observations.

MAKING A CONDUCTIVITY TESTER

A. Use wire to connect the positive terminal of a dry cell to a lamp socket. **CAUTION:** *The bulb is fragile and can break.*

B. Use another wire to connect the negative terminal to the positive terminal of a second dry cell.

C. Connect a third wire to the negative terminal of the second dry cell.

D. Connect a fourth wire to the other terminal of the lamp socket.

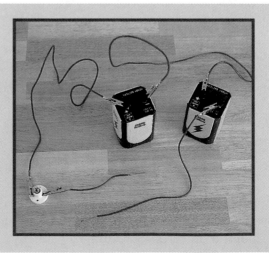

3. Remove the conductivity tester and add a small sample (about a teaspoon) of sodium chloride to the water in the small beaker. Stir with the spoon until mixed.
4. Repeat the conductivity test and record your observations in your data table.
5. Rinse the beaker, spoon, and wire ends with clear water. Then repeat Steps 3 and 4 for each substance provided by your teacher.
   ◆ If the substance is a solid, mix about a teaspoon of it with about 50 mL of fresh water. Test the resulting mixture.
   ◆ If a substance is already liquid, simply pour about 50 mL into the beaker. Test it as you did the solutions.

Analyze and Conclude

1. Why did you test plain water first?
2. Based on your observations, add a column to your chart indicating whether each substance tested contained ionic or covalent bonds.
3. Explain why one substance is a better conductor of electricity than another.
4. Did all the substances that conducted electricity show the same amount of conductivity? How do you know?
5. **Think About It** How might varying the amount of each substance added to the water have affected your results? How could you better control the amount of each substance?

Design an Experiment

Design another experiment to compare a different property of compounds containing ionic and covalent bonds. You might want to examine properties such as whether the substances dissolve in water or in some other liquid. Present your experimental plan to your teacher before proceeding.

SECTION 5 Crystal Chemistry

How Small Do They Get?

1. Place a piece of rock salt on a hard surface. Make a rough sketch of the shape of your sample.

2. Put on your goggles. Then break the piece of salt into several smaller pieces with the back of a metal spoon.

3. Look at these smaller pieces with a hand lens. Then draw a picture of the shapes you see.

4. Crush a few of these smaller pieces with the spoon. Repeat Step 3.

Think It Over
Predicting What do you think the crystals would look like if you crushed them so small that you needed a microscope to see them?

GUIDE FOR READING

◆ How are chemical bonds related to the properties of a mineral?

Reading Tip As you read, make a list of the ways in which a mineral can be described or identified.

A class of earth science students gathers rock samples on a field trip. They want to know if the rocks contain any of the minerals they have been studying. The teacher takes a hammer and strikes one rock. It cracks open to reveal a few small crystals peeking out of the new surface. The crystals are mostly the same shape and have a metallic shine. The teacher tries to scratch one crystal, first with her fingernail and then with a copper penny. Only the penny leaves a mark. By now, the students have enough information to make a first guess about the identity of the crystals. They'll do more tests back in their classroom to be sure the mineral is what they think it is.

Mineral Properties

A **mineral** is a naturally occurring solid that has a crystal structure and a definite chemical composition. A few minerals, such as sulfur and gold, are pure elements. But most minerals are compounds.

Mineralogists, scientists who study minerals, identify minerals by looking at certain properties. These properties include color, shininess, density, crystal shape, hardness, and others. Color and shininess can be observed just by looking at a mineral. Other properties, however, require measurements or testing. For example, scientists rate a mineral's hardness by comparing it with something harder or softer. You can scratch the softest mineral, talc, with your fingernail. Diamond is the hardest mineral. Other minerals are somewhere in between.

Figure 18 The mineral sulfur (above) is a pure element. The mineral galena (right) is a compound of sulfur and lead.

Another key property is the way a mineral breaks apart. Some minerals break into regular shapes. Mica, for example, splits easily along flat surfaces and at sharp angles. Crystals also grow in characteristic shapes. All the properties of a mineral depend on its chemical composition. Since each mineral has a different composition, its properties will not be exactly like those of any other mineral.

☑ *Checkpoint* What is a mineral ?

Bonding in Mineral Crystals

Every mineral has a crystal structure. The repeating pattern of particles creates a shape that may be visible to your eye. Or, you may have to look under a microscope to see it. Either way, the structure of the crystal is a characteristic property of the mineral.

Mineral crystals may be made of ions, or they may contain atoms that are covalently bonded together. **The arrangement of particles in a mineral and the kind of bonds holding them together determine properties such as crystal shape, hardness, and the way the crystal breaks apart.**

An Ionic Crystal In Section 3, you read about halite, a mineral made of sodium chloride (NaCl). You can easily scratch halite with a steel knife. If you put a crystal of halite into water, it would dissolve. The oppositely charged sodium and chloride ions in a halite crystal alternate in every direction, making a pattern something like a three-dimensional checkerboard. This arrangement affects the shape in which halite crystals grow.

If you break a piece of halite, the smaller pieces of halite have the same shape as the bigger piece. When bonds in an ionic crystal break, they break along a line of ions. A blow or crushing action shifts the ions slightly so that positive ions are next to other positive ions and negative ions are next to other negative ions. The effect is the same as bringing the

Figure 19 Mica's flakes **(A)** are a result of how the mineral splits when it breaks. The crystals of fluorite **(B)** and tourmaline **(C)** grew in the shapes you see. *Observing How do the shapes of fluorite crystals and tourmaline crystals differ?*

Figure 20 The particles in an ionic crystal such as halite can shift because of a blow or pressure.

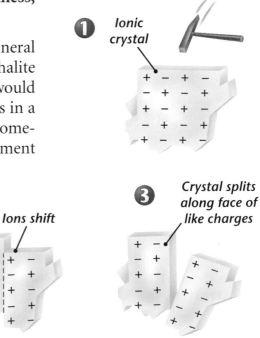

❶ *Ionic crystal*

❷ *Ions shift*

❸ *Crystal splits along face of like charges*

Figure 21 The uneven surfaces on this crystal are typical of broken quartz.
Comparing and Contrasting How does the way quartz breaks compare to the way mica breaks?

north ends of two magnets together. It creates a weakness in the crystal. The ions push each other away, breaking bonds along a flat surface or face. The result is the cube-shaped crystals characteristic of halite.

A Covalent Crystal If you picked up a handful of sand, most likely you would be holding some quartz. Quartz is a common mineral made of silicon and oxygen atoms covalently bonded together (SiO_2). The covalent bonds in quartz are much stronger than the ionic bonds in halite. Quartz won't dissolve in water. You can't scratch it with a knife. In fact, you could use quartz to scratch steel! Because of its strong bonds, a quartz crystal doesn't have clear lines of weakness. You can't crush it into predictable shapes with a hammer. Instead, it breaks into smaller pieces with irregular shapes. The broken surfaces have shell-like ridges similar to chipped glass. These features help identify the mineral as quartz.

Comparing Crystals

Not all mineral crystals made of ions have the same properties as halite. Similarly, not all minerals made of covalently bonded atoms are like quartz. Properties such as hardness, for example, depend on the strength of the bonds in a crystal. The stronger bonds of quartz make it harder than halite. But other crystals with covalently bonded atoms are stronger than quartz. Still others have weaknesses in their bonds that cause the minerals to break apart the same way every time.

Experienced mineralogists can usually identify a mineral just by looking at it. But when there is a question, they test the sample for characteristics such as hardness and the way the crystals break. The results give the answer.

Section 5 Review

1. Name two properties of minerals that depend on chemical bonds.
2. What property of a mineral can be determined by scratching it?
3. How does the way in which a mineral crystal breaks apart help to identify it?
4. **Thinking Critically Comparing and Contrasting** Name three ways in which a halite crystal differs from a quartz crystal.

Science at Home

Construct a model of an ionic crystal. Place spherical objects of two different sizes (such as balls of clay) in a checkerboard pattern to make the first layer. Now place one smaller object on top of a larger one and vice versa to make the second layer. Continue until the first layer is completely covered. Construct a third layer in a similar fashion. Explain to your family how your model represents an ionic crystal.

SECTION 1 Inside an Atom

Key Ideas

◆ An atom consists of a nucleus of protons and neutrons, surrounded by rapidly moving electrons.

◆ Chemical reactions involve the valence electrons of atoms. Chemical bonds form when electrons are transferred or shared between atoms.

Key Terms

nucleus   electron
proton   valence electron
neutron   electron dot diagram

SECTION 2 Atoms in the Periodic Table

Key Ideas

◆ The periodic table organizes the elements according to atomic number.

◆ Families of elements have similar chemical properties.

◆ The noble gases (Group 18) are the least reactive elements. Elements in groups 1 and 17 are highly reactive.

Key Terms

atomic number   period
group   halogen
family

SECTION 3 Ionic Bonds

Key Ideas

◆ Ions form when atoms become charged after gaining or losing electrons.

◆ Ionic compounds exist in the form of crystals made of many ions, each attracted to all the surrounding ions of opposite charge.

◆ Ionic compounds have high melting and boiling points. They conduct electricity when dissolved in water.

Key Terms

ion   polyatomic ion
ionic bond   crystal

SECTION 4 Covalent Bonds

Key Ideas

◆ In covalent bonds, pairs of electrons are shared between atoms.

◆ Some atoms share electrons unequally in a covalent bond, causing bonds to become polar.

◆ Attractions between polar molecules are stronger than attractions between nonpolar molecules, leading to differences in properties.

Key Terms

covalent bond   polar
double bond   nonpolar
molecular compound

SECTION 5 Crystal Chemistry

INTEGRATING EARTH SCIENCE

Key Ideas

◆ Minerals have characteristic properties, such as hardness, density, color, crystal shape, and the way the crystal breaks and grows.

◆ The properties of a mineral depend on its chemical composition and the type of bonds. Mineral crystals may contain ions or covalently bonded atoms.

◆ The stronger the chemical bonds in a mineral crystal, the harder the crystal is.

Key Term

mineral

USING THE INTERNET

www.science-explorer.phschool.com

ACTIVITY

Reviewing Content

For more review of key concepts, see the Interactive Student Tutorial CD-ROM.

Multiple Choice

Choose the letter of the best answer.

1. The atomic number of an atom is determined by the number of
   a. protons.
   b. electrons.
   c. neutrons.
   d. valence electrons.
2. The vertical columns on the periodic table organize elements by
   a. periods.
   b. metals.
   c. families.
   d. nonmetals.
3. When an atom loses an electron, it
   a. becomes a negative ion.
   b. becomes a positive ion.
   c. forms a covalent bond.
   d. gains protons.
4. Which of these is a property of an ionic compound?
   a. low melting point
   b. poor conductor of electricity
   c. crystal shape
   d. shared electrons
5. A chemical bond in which a pair of electrons is shared between two atoms is called
   a. ionic.
   b. covalent.
   c. polyatomic.
   d. triple.

True or False

If the statement is true, write true. If it is false, change the underlined word or words to make the statement true.

6. Using the periodic table, you can determine that a potassium atom has <u>one</u> valence electron.
7. When a chlorine atom gains an electron, it becomes a <u>positive ion</u>.
8. When atoms share electrons unequally, a <u>polar</u> bond forms.
9. Two polar molecules have <u>weaker</u> attractions between them than two nonpolar molecules do.
10. <u>Hardness</u> is determined by how easily a mineral can be scratched.

Checking Concepts

11. Strontium is classified as an alkaline earth metal. Look at the periodic table and name the other elements that are alkaline earth metals.
12. Use the periodic table to identify what type of chemical bond is involved in each of these compounds: NaF, NO_2, CBr_4, MgS. Explain your reasoning.
13. How is a covalent bond between two atoms affected when each atom attracts electrons equally?
14. Of all the elements, fluorine atoms attract electrons most strongly. When fluorine atoms form covalent bonds with other kinds of atoms, are the bonds polar or nonpolar?
15. **Writing to Learn** Imagine you are a chlorine atom. Write a first-person description of the changes you undergo when forming an ionic bond with sodium. Compare these with what happens when you form a covalent bond with another chlorine atom.

Thinking Visually

16. **Venn Diagram** Copy the Venn diagram comparing ionic and molecular compounds onto a separate sheet of paper. Then complete the diagram and add a title. (For more on Venn diagrams, see the Skills Handbook.)

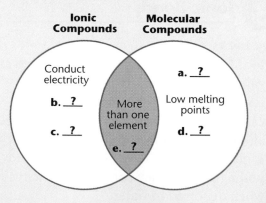

Ionic Compounds — Molecular Compounds

Conduct electricity
a. ?
b. ?
More than one element
Low melting points
c. ?
d. ?
e. ?

Applying Skills

Element X exists as a nonpolar molecule made of two identical atoms. When individual atoms of element X react with sodium, they form ions with a 2– charge. Use the periodic table of the elements in Section 2 or in Appendix D to answer Questions 17–21.

17. **Classifying** To what group of elements does element *X* belong?
18. **Inferring** How many valence electrons does an atom of element *X* have?
19. **Predicting** Sodium can react with element X to form a compound. How many atoms of sodium are needed for each atom of element X? Write the formula for the compound.
20. **Calculating** How many covalent bonds can element *X* form?
21. **Posing Questions** In order to identify element *X*, what additional questions would you need to ask?

Thinking Critically

22. **Problem Solving** Suppose you were given two mineral crystals that looked alike. How would you determine the identity of each?
23. **Inferring** Element Z is a yellow solid that melts at about 100°C and does not conduct electricity. What type of bond holds the element's atoms together? Explain the reasoning for your answer.
24. **Making Generalizations** How does the location of an element on the periodic table help you determine how reactive that element might be?
25. **Applying Concepts** Use the periodic table to find the number of valence electrons for calcium (Ca), aluminum (Al), rubidium (Rb), oxygen (O), sulfur (S), and iodine (I). Then use that information to predict the formula for each of the following compounds: calcium oxide, aluminum iodide, rubidium sulfide, and aluminum oxide.

Performance Assessment

CHAPTER PROJECT 2 — Wrap Up

Present Your Project Before you present your models to the class, use an index card for each model to make a key telling what each part of the model represents. Explain why you chose particular items to model the atoms and the chemical bonds. How are your models alike or different from models of the same compounds made by other students?

Reflect and Record In your journal, compare your models containing ionic bonds with those containing covalent bonds. Which were easier to show? Why? What more would you like to know about atoms that could help improve your models?

Getting Involved

In Your Home Make a list of materials mentioned in this chapter that you might find in your home (such as sugar, salt, vegetable oil, detergent, and so on). Classify each material as an ionic compound or molecular compound. How is each material used in your home? For as many materials as possible, identify how bonding contributes to the properties that make the material useful. Share this information with your family.

CHAPTER
3
Acids, Bases, and Solutions

WHAT'S AHEAD

SECTION 1 Working With Solutions

Discover **What Makes a Mixture a Solution?**
Try This **Does It Dissolve?**
Sharpen Your Skills **Graphing**
Sharpen Your Skills **Controlling Variables**
Skills Lab **Speedy Solutions**

SECTION 2 Describing Acids and Bases

Discover **What Colors Does Litmus Paper Turn?**

SECTION 3 Acids and Bases in Solution

Discover **What Can Cabbage Juice Tell You?**
Try This **pHone Home**
Real-World Lab **The Antacid Test**

PROJECT 3

Make Your Own Indicator

These delicious-looking fruits are more than just nutritious, juicy treats. Most fruits are acidic. And some fruits contain chemicals that change color in an acid or a base. Such chemicals are called acid-base indicators. Parts of many plants are natural acid-base indicators. Flowers, leaves, or the skins of some fruits, for example, can be used to make indicator solutions.

As you learn about acids and bases in this chapter, you can make your own solutions that will tell you if something is an acid or a base. Then you can use your solutions to test for acids and bases among substances found in your home.

Your Goal To make acid-base indicators from flowers, fruits, vegetables, or other common plant materials.

To complete the project you must
- ◆ make one or more indicators that will turn colors in acids and bases
- ◆ use your indicators to test a number of substances
- ◆ compare your indicators to a standard pH scale
- ◆ rank the tested substances according to their pH
- ◆ follow the safety guidelines in Appendix A

Get Started Brainstorm with your classmates about foods, spices, flowers, or other plant materials that have definite, deep colors. Think about fruits and vegetables you may find in a supermarket. These materials are good candidates for your indicators.

Check Your Progress You'll be working on this project as you study this chapter. To keep your project on track, look for Check Your Progress boxes at the following points.

Section Review 2, page 95: Prepare the indicators.
Section Review 3, page 101: Perform the tests.
Section Review 4, page 106: Compare with pH paper.

Wrap Up At the end of the chapter (page 109), you will demonstrate your indicators and rank the tested substances by acidity.

Fruits and fruit juices often contain weak acids.

SECTION 4

Integrating Life Science

Digestion and pH

Discover Where Does Digestion Begin?

SECTION 1 Working With Solutions

DISCOVER • ACTIVITY

What Makes a Mixture a Solution?

1. Put about one quarter of a cup of water into a plastic cup. Add a teaspoon of pepper and stir well.

2. To a second cup of water, add a teaspoon of salt. Stir well.

3. Compare the appearance of the two mixtures.

Think It Over

Observing What is the difference between the two mixtures? What other mixtures have you seen that are similar to pepper and water? That are similar to salt and water?

GUIDE FOR READING

◆ What happens to the particles of a solute when a solution forms?

◆ What factors affect the solubility of a substance?

◆ How do solutes affect the freezing point and boiling point of a solvent?

Reading Tip As you read, make a list of main ideas about solutions.

Imagine a hot summer day. You've been outdoors and now you're really thirsty. A tall, cool glass of just plain water would taste great. Or would it? Have you ever tasted distilled water from the supermarket? It tastes flat. Distilled water is "just plain water." To make it, you boil tap water so it becomes a gas. Then you recollect it as a liquid. This process separates the water from dissolved materials that give it flavor.

Tap water is a mixture of pure water (H_2O) and a variety of other substances, such as chlorine, fluoride, and metallic ions. Gases, such as oxygen and carbon dioxide, are also dissolved in water. Like all mixtures, the composition of tap water can vary. The water coming out of the tap can differ from one home to the next, across a town, or from state to state. Tap water is an example of a kind of mixture called a solution.

Solutions and Suspensions

What happens if you make a mixture of water and pepper? Not much. No matter how much you stir pepper and water, the two never really seem to "mix." When you stop stirring, you can still see pepper flakes floating on the water's surface and collecting at the bottom of the cup. You could scoop them out if you wanted to. Pepper and water make a suspension. A **suspension** (suh SPEN shun) is a mixture in which particles can be seen and easily separated by settling or filtration. If you tasted the pepper suspension, you might find that one mouthful of it tastes peppery, but another mouthful does not. Such a mixture is not evenly mixed.

On the other hand, if you stir salt into water, the salt disappears. Water and salt form a **solution,** a well-mixed mixture. If you taste a salt solution, any sip tastes just as salty as the next. A solution has the same properties throughout. The particles of a solution are much smaller than those of a suspension. Solutions and suspensions also differ in the way the parts of the mixture can be separated. The particles in a solution are too small to see. You cannot separate salt from water by filtering it or by letting it settle. Boiling the water away, however, will work. Letting the water evaporate will also separate the salt.

Solvents and Solutes

All solutions have at least two parts: the solvent and the solute. The **solvent** is the part of a solution present in the largest amount. It dissolves the other substances. A substance that is present in a solution in a smaller amount and dissolved by the solvent is the **solute.** In salt water, the solvent is water and the solute is salt.

Water as a Solvent In many common solutions, the solvent is water. Sugar in water, for example, is the starting solution for flavored soft drinks. Adding food coloring gives the drink color. Dissolving carbon dioxide gas in the mixture produces a soda. Water dissolves so many substances that it is often called the "universal solvent."

INTEGRATING LIFE SCIENCE Water solutions are essential in the living world. Cells are made mostly of water and dissolved chemicals. The chemicals needed for life react best in solution. For example, the digestion of food by living things happens in water solutions. And water solutions in the soil contain nutrients used by plants.

Figure 1 Glitter mixes with the water when you shake the paperweight, but settles out later. *Classifying Are the glitter particles in solution or in suspension?*

Figure 2 When air bubbles are blown through a fish tank, oxygen gas dissolves in the water. Fish take in this oxygen through their gills. Without oxygen, the fish would die.

Figure 3 Solutions can be made from any combination of the three states of matter. *Interpreting Tables* In which of these solutions is the solvent a substance other than water?

Examples of Common Solutions		
Solute	**Solvent**	**Solution**
Gas	Gas	Air (oxygen and other gases in nitrogen)
Gas	Liquid	Soda water (carbon dioxide in water)
Liquid	Liquid	Antifreeze (ethylene glycol and water)
Solid	Liquid	Dental filling (silver in mercury)
Solid	Liquid	Ocean water (sodium chloride and other compounds in water)
Solid	Solid	Brass (zinc and copper)

Solutions Without Water Many solutions are made with solvents other than water. For example, gasoline is a solution of several different liquid fuels. You don't even need a liquid solvent to make solutions. A solution may be made of any combination of gases, liquids, or solids.

Particles in a Solution

Why do solutes seem to disappear when you mix them with water? If you had a microscope powerful enough to look at the particles in the mixture, what would you see? **Whenever a solution forms, particles of the solute leave each other and become surrounded by particles of the solvent.**

Ionic Solids in Water Figure 4 shows what happens when an ionic solid mixes with water. The positive and negative ions are attracted to polar water molecules. Water molecules surround each ion as it leaves the surface of the crystal. Eventually all the ions go into solution.

Figure 4 Water molecules surround and separate positive and negative ions as an ionic solid dissolves. Notice that sodium ions attract the oxygen ends of the water molecules.

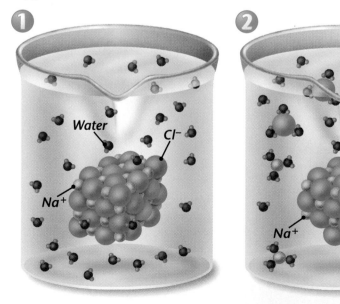

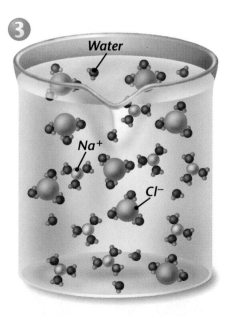

Molecular Solids in Water Not every substance breaks into ions when it dissolves in water. A molecular solid, such as sugar, breaks up into individual neutral molecules. The polar water molecules attract the slightly polar sugar molecules. This causes the sugar molecules to move away from each other. But covalent bonds within the molecules are undisturbed. Like ions, the sugar molecules become surrounded by water.

Solutions and Conductivity You have a solution, but you don't know if it was made with salt or sugar in water. How could you use what you know about particles to find out? (Remember, a smart scientist never tastes chemicals!) Think about what you learned about the electrical conductivity of compounds. Ionic compounds dissolved in water conduct electricity, but molecular compounds do not. You could test the conductivity of the solution. If no ions were present (as in a sugar solution), electricity would not flow.

✓ *Checkpoint* *How do ionic and molecular solids differ from each other in solution?*

Concentration

Suppose you make two cups of hot herbal tea. You leave a tea bag in the first cup for fifteen seconds. You put another tea bag in the second cup for a few minutes. When you're done, the tea in the second cup is darker than the tea in the first cup.

The two cups of tea differ in their concentrations. That is, they differ in the amount of solute (tea) dissolved in a certain amount of solvent (water). Chemists describe the first mixture as a **dilute solution** because only a little solute is dissolved in the water. By comparison, the darker tea is a **concentrated solution** because it has more solute dissolved in the water.

Figure 5 Weak tea is a dilute solution, whereas strong tea is a more concentrated solution.

Solubility in 100 g Water at 0°C	
Compound	Solubility (g)
Salt (NaCl)	35.7
Baking soda (NaHCO$_3$)	6.9
Carbon dioxide (CO$_2$)	0.348
Sugar (C$_{12}$H$_{22}$O$_{11}$)	180

Figure 6 Each compound listed in the table dissolves in water, but they have different solubilities.
Comparing and Contrasting Which compound is the most soluble? Which is the least soluble?

Solubility

If a substance dissolves in water, a question you might ask is, "How well does it dissolve?" Suppose you add sugar to a glass of iced tea. You could add half a teaspoon to make it taste slightly sweet. Or, you could add two teaspoons to make it sweeter. Is there a limit to how "sweet" you can make the tea? Yes. At the temperature of iced tea, three or four teaspoons of sugar are about all you can add. No matter how much you stir the tea, no more sugar will dissolve. **Solubility** is a measure of how well a solute can dissolve in a solvent at a given temperature.

When you've added so much solute that no more dissolves, you have a **saturated solution.** Any more sugar would just fall to the bottom of the glass and not make the tea any sweeter. On the other hand, if you can continue to dissolve more solute, you still have an **unsaturated solution.**

The solubility of a substance tells you the limit on how much you can add before you make a saturated solution. Because solubility is a characteristic property of matter, you can use it to help identify a compound. The solubility of a substance is usually described for a specific solvent (such as water) and under certain conditions (such as temperature). Figure 6 compares the solubilities of some familiar compounds when they dissolve in water.

From the table you can see that 35.7 g of salt will dissolve in 100 g of water at 0°C. But the same mass of water at the same temperature will dissolve 180 g of sugar! If you had two white powders, you could use solubility to tell the difference without tasting them.

☑ *Checkpoint* Why doesn't solute added to a saturated solution dissolve?

Changing Solubility

Which holds more sugar: iced tea or hot tea? You have already read that there is a limit on solubility. An iced tea and sugar solution quickly becomes saturated. Yet a hot, steaming cup of the same tea can hold several more teaspoons of sugar before the limit is reached. Later, if the solution is cooled, the solubility of sugar decreases. Sugar crystals will form. The solubilities of sugar and other substances change when conditions change. **Among the factors that affect the solubility of a substance are temperature and type of solvent.**

Figure 7 Rock candy is made by dissolving sugar in hot water. As the sugar water cools, sugar crystals collect on a string.

Figure 8 Has this ever happened to you? Opening a bottle of soda water can sometimes produce quite a spray as dissolved gas comes out of solution. *Relating Cause and Effect Why does more gas escape from a warm bottle of soda water than from a cold bottle?*

Temperature Sugar is one of many solids that dissolve better when the temperature of the solvent increases. Cooks apply this principle to prepare certain foods. A cook cannot dissolve enough sugar at room temperature to make candy or fudge. The cook must heat the liquid mixture to dissolve the sugar. Later, when the food cools, it will taste sweeter than if it were made at room temperature.

Unlike most solids, gases become less soluble when the temperature goes up. For example, more carbon dioxide will dissolve in cold water than in hot water. Carbon dioxide makes soda water fizzy when you pour it into a glass. If you open a warm bottle of soda water, carbon dioxide escapes the liquid in greater amounts than if the soda water had been chilled. Why does warm soda taste "flat"? It contains less gas. If you like soda water that's very fizzy, open it when it's cold!

Solvents If you've ever shaken a bottle of salad dressing, you've seen how quickly water and oil separate. This is because water is polar and oil is nonpolar. Polar compounds and nonpolar compounds do not mix very well. For liquid solutions, the solvent affects how well a solute dissolves. The expression "like dissolves like" gives you a clue to which solutes are soluble in which solvents. Ionic and polar compounds dissolve in polar solvents. Nonpolar compounds do not dissolve in polar solvents. If you work with paints, you know that water-based (latex) paints can be cleaned up with just soap and water. But oil-based paints may require cleanup with a nonpolar solvent, such as turpentine.

Graphing The table below shows how many grams of potassium nitrate (KNO_3) can dissolve in 100 g of water at different temperatures. Use the data to make a graph. Label the horizontal axis *Temperature* and the vertical axis *Solubility*.

Temperature (°C)	Solubility (g/100g H_2O)
0	13
20	31
40	65
60	108
80	164
100	247

What does the graph show?

Sharpen your Skills

Controlling Variables

How does the mass of a solute affect the boiling temperature of water? Design an experiment using a solute, water, a balance, a hot plate, and a thermometer.

What variables should remain constant in your experiment? What is the manipulated variable? What will be the responding variable?

With approval from your teacher, do the experiment. Report on your results.

Effects of Solutes on Solutions

Have you ever made ice cream? First you mix cream, sugar, and other ingredients. Then you freeze the mixture by packing it in ice and water. But ice water by itself is not cold enough to do the job. Cream freezes at a temperature lower than the freezing point of water (0°C). Adding salt to the ice water creates a mixture that is several degrees cooler. This salty ice water is cold enough to freeze the cream. Mmm!

You can use salt to affect boiling, too. When cooking spaghetti, people often add table salt to the water. As a result, the water boils at a temperature higher than 100°C, the boiling point of water. Just two teaspoons of salt for each quart of water will raise the boiling point about 1°C. So, if you add a *tablespoon* or so of salt to a pot of water, the boiling temperature will increase by a few degrees. This change is enough to cook the spaghetti faster.

Why does salt make cold water colder when it freezes and hot water hotter when it boils? The answer to both parts of this question depends on solute particles.

Lower Freezing Points **Solutes lower the freezing point of a solvent.** When liquid water freezes, the molecules stop moving about. Instead, they form crystals of solid ice. Look at Figure 9 to compare the particles in pure water with those in a saltwater solution. Notice that pure water is made only of water molecules. In the salt solution, solute particles are present, too. In fact, they're in the way. The solute particles make it harder for the water molecules to form crystals. The temperature must drop lower than 0°C for a solid to form.

Figure 9 The freezing point and boiling point of water are affected by the presence of solute particles. Solute particles interfere with the change of state.

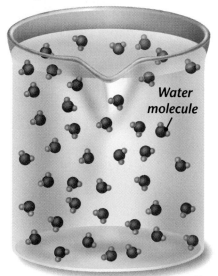

Pure liquid water

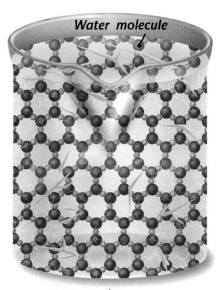

Ice

Salt water

Higher Boiling Points Solutes raise the boiling point of a solvent. To see why, think about the difference between the molecules of a liquid and those of a gas. In a liquid, molecules are moving close to each other. In a gas, they are far apart and moving much more rapidly. As the temperature of a liquid rises, the molecules gain energy and escape into the air. Now compare the left and right solutions in Figure 9 again. In pure water, all the molecules are water. In the solution, however, some of the particles are water molecules and others are particles of solute. The presence of the solute makes it harder for the water molecules to escape, so more energy is needed. The temperature must go higher than 100°C for the water to boil.

Figure 10 The coolant in a car radiator is a solution.
Predicting On a very cold day, what might happen to a car that had only water in the radiator?

![INTEGRATING TECHNOLOGY] Car manufacturers make use of the effects of solutes to protect engines from heat and cold. The coolant in a car radiator is a solution of water and another liquid called antifreeze. Often the antifreeze is ethylene glycol, which freezes at –13°C and boils at 176°C. The mixture of the two liquids has a lower freezing point and higher boiling point than either liquid alone. This solution safely absorbs heat given off by the running engine. Risk of damage to the car from overheating is greatly reduced. So is the risk of damage from freezing in very cold weather.

Section 1 Review

1. Describe what happens to the molecules of a solid, such as a sugar cube, when it dissolves in water. How does the process differ for an ionic compound, such as table salt?
2. Why would an ionic compound be more likely to dissolve in water than in oil?
3. Why does salt sprinkled on icy roads cause the ice to melt?
4. **Thinking Critically Relating Cause and Effect** Why is the temperature needed to freeze ocean water lower than the temperature needed to freeze the surface of a freshwater lake?

Science at Home

With your family, make a saturated solution of baking soda in water. Add one teaspoon of baking soda to about a cup of cool water. Stir until the baking soda dissolves. Continue adding baking soda in this manner until no more dissolves. Keep track of how much baking soda you use. Then ask your family to predict what would happen if you used warm water instead. Test their predictions and compare the results with those of the first test.

Speedy Solutions

I n this lab, you will design an experiment to find out how a chosen variable affects the speed at which salt dissolves in water.

Problem

How can you control the rate at which salt dissolves in water?

Suggested Materials

spoon	solid stoppers, #4
thermometers	hot plate
balance	stirring rods
ice	timer or watch
test tube rack	test tubes, 25×150 mm

coarse, rock, and table salt

graduated cylinders and beakers, various sizes

Design a Plan

1. Make a list of all the variables you can think of that could affect the speed with which salt dissolves in water.
2. Compare your list with your classmates' lists, and add other variables.
3. Choose one variable from your list to test.
4. Write a hypothesis predicting the effect of your chosen variable on the speed of dissolving.
5. Decide how to work with your choice.
   ◆ If you choose temperature, you might perform tests at 10°C, 20°C, 30°C, 40°C, and 50°C.
   ◆ If you choose stirring, you might stir for various amounts of time.
6. Plan at least three tests for whichever variable you choose. Remember to control all other variables.
7. Write down a series of steps for your procedure and safety guidelines for your experiment. Be quite detailed in your plan.
8. As part of your procedure, prepare a data table in which to record your results. Fill in the headings on your table that identify your manipulated variable and the responding variable. (*Hint:* Remember to include units.)
9. Have your teacher approve your procedure, safety guidelines, and data table.
10. Perform the experiment.

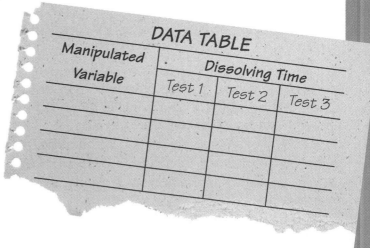

Manipulated Variable	DATA TABLE Dissolving Time		
	Test 1	Test 2	Test 3

Analyze and Conclude

1. Which is the manipulated variable in your experiment? Which is the responding variable? How do you know which is which?
2. List three variables you held constant in your procedure. Explain why controlling these variables makes your data more reliable.
3. Make a line graph of your data. Label the horizontal axis with the manipulated variable. Label the vertical axis with the responding variable. Use an appropriate scale for each axis and label the units.
4. Study the shape of your graph. Write a conclusion about the effect of the variable you tested on the speed of salt dissolving in water.
5. Does your conclusion support the hypothesis you wrote in Step 4? Explain.
6. How do your results relate to what you have learned about particles and solubility?
7. What advantage would there be in running your tests a second or third time?
8. **Think About It** If you switched procedures with another student who tested the same variable as you, do you think you would get the same results? Explain why or why not.

More to Explore

Choose another variable from the list you made in Steps 1 and 2. Repeat the process with that variable. Of the two variables you chose, which was easier to work with? Explain.

What Colors Does Litmus Paper Turn?

1. [icons] Use a plastic dropper to put a drop of lemon juice on a clean piece of red litmus paper. Put another drop on a clean piece of blue litmus paper. Observe.

2. Rinse your dropper with water. Then test other substances the same way. You might test orange juice, ammonia cleaner, tap water, vinegar, and solutions of soap, baking soda, and table salt. Record all your observations.

3. Wash your hands when you are finished.

Think It Over

Classifying Group the substances based on how they make the litmus paper change color. Do you notice any other characteristics that the members of each group have in common?

GUIDE FOR READING

◆ What properties can you use to identify acids?

◆ What properties can you use to identify bases?

Reading Tip Before you read, preview *Exploring Uses of Acids* and *Exploring Uses of Bases*. List examples of acids and bases you are already familiar with.

D id you eat any fruit for breakfast today—perhaps an orange, an apple, or fruit juice? If so, an acid was part of your meal. The last time you washed your hair, did you use shampoo? If your answer is yes, then you may have used a base.

You use many products that contain acids and bases. Manufacturers, farmers, and builders depend on acids and bases in their work. The chemical reactions of acids and bases even keep you alive! What are acids and bases? How do they react, and what are their uses? In this section you will start to find out.

Properties of Acids

What is an acid and how do you know when you have one? Test its properties. **Acids** are compounds that share characteristic properties in the kinds of reactions they undergo. **An acid is a substance that tastes sour, reacts with metals and carbonates, and turns blue litmus red.**

Sour Taste If you've ever tasted a lemon, you've had firsthand experience with the sour taste of acids. Can you think of other foods that sometimes taste sour, or tart? Citrus fruits—lemons, grapefruits, oranges, and limes—are acidic. They all contain citric acid. Other fruits (cherries, tomatoes, apples) contain acids also. The vinegar used in salad dressing is made from a solution of water and acetic acid. Tea is acidic, too. So is sour milk, but you might not want to drink it!

Figure 11 A sour taste means that food is acidic.

Although sour taste is a common characteristic of acids, it is not one that you would use to identify a compound as an acid. Scientists never taste chemicals in order to identify them. Though sour foods may be safe to eat, many other acids are not.

Reactions With Metals Do you notice bubbles in Figure 13? Acids react with certain metals to produce hydrogen gas. Not all metals react this way, but magnesium, zinc, and iron do. When they react, the metals seem to disappear in the solution. This observation is one reason acids are described as **corrosive,** meaning they "eat away" at other materials.

INTEGRATING TECHNOLOGY The metal plate in Figure 13 is being etched with acid. Etching is one method of making printing plates that are then used to print works of art on paper. To make an etching, an artist first coats a metal plate with an acid-resistant material—often beeswax. Then the design is cut into the beeswax with a sharp tool, exposing some of the metal. When the plate is treated with acid, the acid eats away the design in the exposed metal. Later, ink applied to the plate collects in the grooves made by the acid. The ink is transferred to the paper when the etching is printed.

Some Important Acids	
Acid	**Formula**
Hydrochloric acid	HCl
Nitric acid	HNO_3
Sulfuric acid	H_2SO_4
Carbonic acid	H_2CO_3
Acetic acid	$HC_2H_3O_2$
Phosphoric acid	H_3PO_4

Figure 12 The table lists the names and formulas of some common acids.

Figure 13 Metal etching takes advantage of the reaction of an acid with a metal. Lines are cut in the wax coating on the plate. Here, hydrochloric acid eats away at the exposed zinc metal, forming bubbles you can see in the close-up. *Applying Concepts What gas forms in this reaction?*

Putting someone to the "acid test" has nothing to do with litmus. The phrase is a figure of speech. It refers to a situation that tries someone's character, ability, courage, or other personal qualities. It comes from an old use of nitric acid to test the purity of gold. Many metals react with acid, but gold does not. Fake gold corrodes, while the value and quality of real gold are revealed.

In Your Journal

Write about a time you or someone you know went through an "acid test." What was hard about the situation? What did you learn from it about yourself or the other person?

Reactions With Carbonates Acids also react with carbonate ions in a characteristic way. Carbonate ions contain carbon and oxygen atoms bonded together. They also carry an overall negative charge (CO_3^{2-}). When acids react with compounds made of carbonates, a gas forms. In this case, the gas is carbon dioxide.

INTEGRATING EARTH SCIENCE Geologists, scientists who study Earth, use the reaction of acids with carbonates to identify limestone. Limestone is made of calcium carbonate ($CaCO_3$). If a dilute solution of hydrochloric acid (HCl) is poured on a limestone rock, bubbles of carbon dioxide appear. Look at the equation for this reaction.

$$2\ HCl + CaCO_3 \rightarrow CaCl_2 + CO_2 + H_2O$$

This reaction is used to determine if different materials are limestone. Coral reefs are a form of limestone found in the ocean. The reefs are large structures made by millions of tiny sea animals that produce an outer covering of calcium carbonate. Chalk is another form of limestone. It forms from the hard parts of microscopic sea animals, deposited in thick layers. Over time, these layers are pressed together and harden to form chalk.

Reactions With Indicators If you did the Discover activity, you used litmus paper to test several substances. Litmus is an example of an **indicator,** a compound that changes color in the presence of an acid or a base. Vinegar and lemon juice turn blue litmus paper red. In fact, acids always turn litmus paper red. Sometimes chemists use other indicators to test for acids, but litmus is one of the easiest to use.

✓ *Checkpoint* *What is the purpose of using an indicator?*

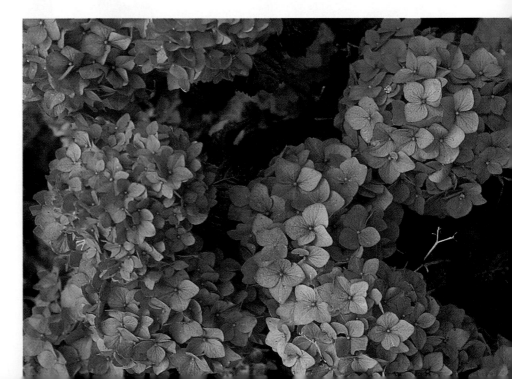

Figure 14 Hydrangea flowers are natural indicators. They may range in color from bright pink to blue, depending on the acidity of the soil in which the bush grows.

EXPLORING Uses of Acids

A cids play important roles in the chemistry of living things. Acids also are used to make valuable products for homes, farms, and industries.

Acids and food
Many of the vitamins in the foods you eat are acids.

Acids in the body
Acids are useful in the body and are also waste products of cell processes.

Acid in the stomach helps to digest protein.

During exercise, lactic acid builds up in hard-working muscles.

Oranges and tomatoes contain ascorbic acid, or vitamin C.

Folic acid, needed for healthy cell growth, is found in green leafy vegetables.

Acid

In solution, acids often look just like water, but they react very differently. A concentrated acid can burn a hole in metal, cloth, skin, wood, and other materials.

Acids in the home
People often use dilute solutions of acids to clean brick and other surfaces. Hardware stores sell muriatic (hydrochloric) acid, which is used to clean bricks and metals.

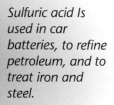

Acids and industry
Farmers and manufacturers depend on acids for many uses.

Sulfuric acid Is used in car batteries, to refine petroleum, and to treat iron and steel.

Nitric acid and phosphoric acid are used to make fertilizers for crops, lawns, and gardens.

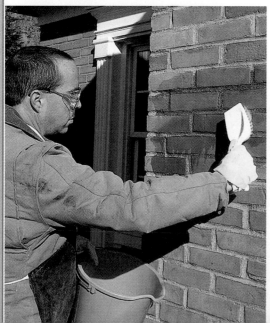

EXPLORING Uses of Bases

The reactions of bases make them valuable raw materials for a range of products.

Bases and food
Baking soda reacts with acids to produce carbon dioxide gas in baked goods. Without these gas bubbles, this delicious variety of breads, biscuits, cakes, and cookies would not be light and fluffy.

Bases in the home
Ammonia solutions are safe to spray with bare hands, but gloves must be worn when working with drain cleaners.

Drain cleaners contain sodium hydroxide (lye).

You can't mistake the odor of household cleaning products made with ammonia.

In solution, bases sometimes look like water, or they may be cloudy white. Strong bases can burn your skin.

Base

Bases and industry
Mortar and cement are manufactured using the bases calcium oxide and calcium hydroxide. Gardeners sometimes add calcium oxide to soil to make the soil less acidic for plants.

Bases and health
Bases such as milk of magnesia (magnesium hydroxide) and calcium carbonate help ease effects of too much stomach acid.

Properties of Bases

Bases are another group of compounds that can be identified by their common properties. **A base is a substance that tastes bitter, feels slippery, and turns red litmus blue.** Bases often are described as the "opposites" of acids.

Bitter Taste   Have you ever tasted tonic water? The slightly bitter taste is caused by the base quinine. Bases taste bitter. Soaps, some shampoos, and detergents taste bitter too, but you wouldn't want to test them that way.

Slippery Feel   Picture yourself washing your hands. You reach for a bar of soap and rub it between your hands underwater. Think about how slippery your hands feel. This slippery feeling is another characteristic of bases. But just as you avoid tasting a substance to identify it, you wouldn't want to touch it. Strong bases can irritate or burn your skin. A safer way to identify bases is by their other properties.

Reactions With Indicators   As you might guess, if litmus paper can be used to test acids, it can be used to test bases too. Bases turn red litmus blue. Like acids, bases react with other indicators. But litmus paper gives a reliable, safe test. An easy way to remember which color litmus turns for acids or bases is to remember the letter *b*. **B**ases turn litmus paper **b**lue.

Reactions of Bases   Unlike acids, bases don't react with metals or carbonates. At first, you may think it is useless to know that a base doesn't react with certain chemicals. But if you know what a compound *doesn't* do, you know something about it. For example, you know it's not an acid. Another important property of bases is how they react with acids. You will learn more about these reactions in Section 3.

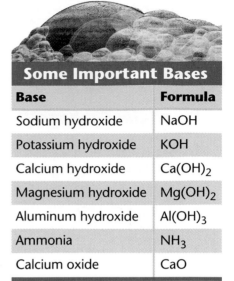

Some Important Bases	
Base	**Formula**
Sodium hydroxide	NaOH
Potassium hydroxide	KOH
Calcium hydroxide	$Ca(OH)_2$
Magnesium hydroxide	$Mg(OH)_2$
Aluminum hydroxide	$Al(OH)_3$
Ammonia	NH_3
Calcium oxide	CaO

Figure 15 The table lists the names and formulas of some common bases.
Predicting What color would any of these compounds turn litmus paper?

Section 2 Review

1. How can you use litmus paper to distinguish an acid from a base?
2. How can you tell if a food may contain an acid or a base as one of its ingredients?
3. Name at least two ways that acids and bases are useful around your home.
4. **Thinking Critically Comparing and Contrasting**   Make a table that compares at least three properties of acids and bases.

Check Your Progress

CHAPTER PROJECT 3

Select sources for your indicators. Explore ways to crush each material and squeeze out its juice. You may have to add some water and remove any solid. (*Hint:* Refrigerate any samples you are not going to use immediately.) Write down your procedure and get your teacher's approval before preparing your indicators.

SECTION
3 Acids and Bases in Solution

DISCOVER

What Can Cabbage Juice Tell You?

1. Using a dropper, put five drops of red cabbage juice into each of three separate plastic cups.

2. Add 10 drops of lemon juice (an acid) to one cup. Add 10 drops of ammonia cleaner (a base) to another. Keep the third cup for comparison. Record the colors you see.

3. Now add ammonia, one drop at a time, to the cup containing lemon juice. Keep adding ammonia until the color no longer changes. Record all color changes you see.

4. Add lemon juice a drop at a time to the ammonia until the color no longer changes. Record the changes you see.

Think It Over
Forming Operational Definitions
Based on your observations, how could you expand your definitions of acids and bases?

GUIDE FOR READING

◆ What kind of ions do acids and bases form in water?
◆ What does pH tell you about a solution?
◆ What happens in a neutralization reaction?

Reading Tip As you read, write one sentence to summarize the main idea discussed under each heading.

Figure 16 You can find at least one hydrogen atom in the formula of each of these acids.

Acid Formulas	
Name	**Formula**
Hydrochloric acid	HCl
Nitric acid	HNO_3
Sulfuric acid	H_2SO_4
Acetic acid	$HC_2H_3O_2$

A chemist pours hydrochloric acid into a beaker. Then she adds sodium hydroxide to the acid. The mixture looks the same, but the beaker becomes warm. If she tested the solution with litmus paper, what color would the paper turn? Would you be surprised if it did not turn color at all? If *exactly* the right amounts and concentrations of the acid and the base were mixed, the beaker would hold nothing but salt water! How could those two harmful chemicals react to produce something harmless? In this section, you will find the answer.

Acids in Solution

What do acids have in common? Notice that all the formulas in Figure 16 begin with hydrogen. The acids you will learn about are made of one or more hydrogen ions and a negative ion. A **hydrogen ion (H^+)** is an atom of hydrogen that has lost its electron. The negative ion may be a nonmetal or a polyatomic ion. But the key piece of an acid is the hydrogen ion.

Acids in water solution separate into hydrogen ions (H^+) and negative ions. In the case of hydrochloric acid, hydrogen ions and chloride ions (Cl^-) form.

$$HCl \xrightarrow{water} H^+ + Cl^-$$

If another acid were substituted for HCl, the negative ions would be different. But hydrogen ions would be produced in each case.

90**96 ◆ L**

Figure 17 All acids share certain chemical and physical properties when dissolved in water. Most acids are very soluble.

Now you can add to the definition of acids you learned in Section 2. **An acid is any substance that forms hydrogen ions (H^+) in water.** These hydrogen ions cause the properties of acids you can see. For instance, when you add certain metals to an acid, hydrogen ions interact with the metal atoms. One product of the reaction is hydrogen gas (H_2). Hydrogen ions also react with blue litmus paper, turning it red. That's why every acid gives the same litmus test result.

Bases in Solution

The formulas of bases give you clues to what ions they have in common. Look at Figure 18. Many bases are made of positive ions combined with hydroxide ions. The **hydroxide ion (OH^-)** is polyatomic, made of oxygen and hydrogen. It has a negative charge.

When bases dissolve in water, the positive ions and hydroxide ions separate. Look, for example, at what happens to sodium hydroxide:

$$NaOH \xrightarrow{water} Na^+ + OH^-$$

Not every base contains hydroxide. For example, the gas ammonia (NH_3) does not. But in solution, ammonia reacts with water to form hydroxide ions.

$$NH_3 + H_2O \rightarrow NH_4^+ + OH^-$$

Notice that in both reactions, there are positive ions and negative hydroxide ions. These examples give you another way to define bases. **A base is any substance that forms hydroxide ions (OH^-) in water.** Hydroxide ions are responsible for the bitter taste and slippery feel of bases. Hydroxides also turn red litmus blue.

☑ *Checkpoint* What is a hydroxide ion made of?

Figure 18 Many, but not all, bases dissolve well in water. *Making Generalizations What do all of the base formulas in the table have in common?*

Base Formulas	
Name	**Formula**
Sodium hydroxide	NaOH
Potassium hydroxide	KOH
Calcium hydroxide	Ca(OH)$_2$
Magnesium hydroxide	Mg(OH)$_2$

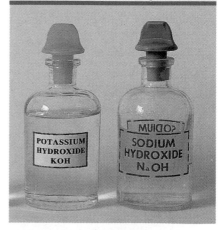

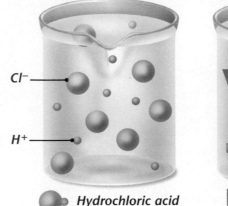
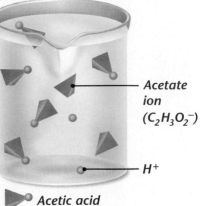

Figure 19 In a solution of a strong acid, all the acid molecules break up into ions. In a solution of a weak acid, however, fewer molecules do so.

Cl⁻

H⁺

Acetate ion ($C_2H_3O_2^-$)

H⁺

Hydrochloric acid

Acetic acid

pHone Home

ACTIVITY

Find out the pH of familiar substances in your home.

1. Put on your safety goggles and apron.

2. Select substances such as fruit juices, soda water, coffee, tea, or antacids.

3. Predict which substances are most acidic or most basic.

4. If the sample is solid, dissolve some in a cup of water. Use a liquid as is.

5. Using a plastic dropper, transfer a drop of each sample onto a fresh strip of paper for testing pH.

6. Compare the color of the strip to the pH values on the package.

7. Repeat for all your samples. Remember to rinse the dropper between tests.

Interpreting Data List the samples from lowest to highest pH. Which results, if any, surprised you?

Strengths of Acids and Bases

Acids and bases may be strong or weak. Strength refers to how well an acid or base separates into ions in water. In a strong acid, most of the molecules break up into ions in solution. In a weak acid, fewer molecules break up into ions. At the same concentrations, strong acids produce more H⁺ ions than weak acids. Examples of strong acids include hydrochloric acid, sulfuric acid, and nitric acid. Most other acids, such as acetic acid, are weak acids.

Similarly, strong bases break up in solution. They produce more OH⁻ ions than equal concentrations of weak bases. Ammonia is a weak base. Lye, or sodium hydroxide, is a strong base.

Strength determines, in part, how safe acids and bases are to use. For example, all the acids that are safe to eat, such as acetic acid and citric acid, are weak. Ammonia cleaner may irritate your hands slightly if you use it. But the same concentration of drain cleaner, which contains sodium hydroxide, would burn your skin.

People often say that a solution is weak when they mean it is dilute. This could be a dangerous mistake! Even a dilute solution of hydrochloric acid can eat a hole in your clothing or sting your skin. An equal concentration of acetic acid would not.

✓ *Checkpoint* *How would a weak base differ from an equal concentration of a strong base in solution?*

Measuring pH

Knowing the concentration of hydrogen ions is the key to knowing how acidic or basic a solution is. To find out the concentration of ions, chemists use a measuring scale called pH. The **pH scale** is a series of numbers from 0 to 14. It measures the concentration of hydrogen ions in a solution.

Figure 20 shows where some familiar substances fit on the pH scale. Notice that the most acidic substances are at the low end of the scale. At the same time, the most basic substances are at the high end of the scale. You need to remember one important point about pH. **When the pH is low, the concentration of hydrogen ions is high.** If you keep this idea in mind, you can make sense of how the scale works.

You can find the pH of a solution by using indicators. The student in Figure 20 is using indicator paper that turns a different color for each pH value. Matching the color of the paper with the colors on the test scale tells how acidic or basic the solution is. A pH lower than 7 is acidic. A pH higher than 7 is basic. If the pH is 7, the solution is neutral. That means it's neither an acid nor a base. Pure water has a pH of 7.

A concentrated solution of acetic acid can have a lower pH than a dilute solution of hydrochloric acid. In order to handle acids and bases safely, you need to know both their pH and their concentration.

Figure 20 The pH scale helps classify solutions as acidic or basic. Indicator paper turns a different color for each pH value. *Interpreting Diagrams If a solution has a pH of 9, is it acidic or basic? What can you say about a solution with a pH of 3?*

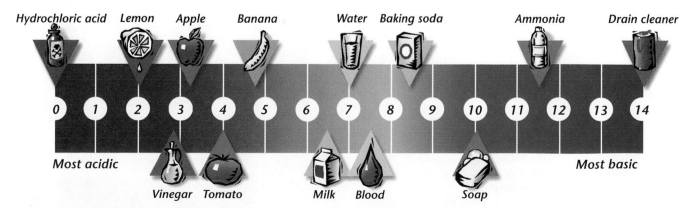

Hydrochloric acid　Lemon　Apple　Banana　Water　Baking soda　Ammonia　Drain cleaner

0　1　2　3　4　5　6　7　8　9　10　11　12　13　14

Most acidic　　　　　　　　　　　　　　　　　　　*Most basic*

Vinegar　Tomato　Milk　Blood　Soap

Figure 21 The trees in this forest show the damaging effects of acid rain.

Acid Rain

Normal rainfall is slightly acidic, with a pH of approximately 5.5.

INTEGRATING ENVIRONMENTAL SCIENCE This acidity comes from carbon dioxide in the air. Carbon dioxide dissolves in rainwater, producing carbonic acid, a weak acid.

$$H_2O + CO_2 \rightarrow H_2CO_3$$

Acid rain is more acidic than normal rainwater. It has a pH as low as 3.5 to 3.0. The extra acidity comes from nitrogen oxides and sulfur oxides. These gases are released into the air as pollutants from industry and motor vehicles. These oxides react with water in the air to produce acids, including nitric acid and sulfuric acid. Rainwater containing these acids has more hydrogen ions. It has a lower pH and is more corrosive. Acid rain can damage statues and buildings, destroy forests, and kill fishes in lakes.

Acid-Base Reactions

The story at the start of this section describes a chemist who mixed hydrochloric acid with sodium hydroxide. She got a solution of table salt (sodium chloride) and water.

$$HCl + NaOH \rightarrow H_2O + Na^+ + Cl^-$$

If you tested the pH of the mixture, it would be close to 7, or neutral. In fact, a reaction between an acid and a base is called a **neutralization** (noo truh lih ZAY shun). As a result of neutralization, an acid-base mixture is not as acidic or basic as the individual starting solutions were.

Sometimes a neutralization reaction results in a neutral solution with a pH of 7. But not always. The pH of the product depends on which acid and base react and how much of each is used. If a small amount of a strong acid is added to a larger amount of strong base, what would be the pH of the mixture? Common sense tells you it would be higher than 7, still somewhat basic.

Figure 22 The solution on the left is acidic. The solution on the right is basic. When mixed, these solutions produced the neutral solution in the center. *Interpreting Photos What tells you if the solution is an acid, a base, or neutral?*

Acidic   Neutral   Basic

Some Salts and Their Uses		
Salt	**Formula**	**Uses**
Sodium chloride	NaCl	Food flavoring; preservative
Potassium iodide	KI	Additive in "iodized" salt that prevents iodine deficiency (goiter)
Calcium chloride	$CaCl_2$	De-icer for roads and walkways
Potassium chloride	KCl	Salt substitute in foods
Calcium carbonate	$CaCO_3$	Found in limestone and sea shells
Ammonium nitrate	NH_4NO_3	Fertilizer; active ingredient in some cold packs

Products of Acid-Base Reactions

"Salt" may be the familiar name of the stuff you sprinkle on food. But to a chemist, the word refers to a specific group of compounds. A **salt** is any ionic compound that can form from the neutralization of an acid with a base. A salt is made of the positive ion of a base and the negative ion of an acid. Look at the equation for the reaction of nitric acid with potassium hydroxide:

$$HNO_3 + KOH \rightarrow H_2O + K^+ + NO_3^-$$

One product of the reaction is water. The other product is potassium nitrate (KNO_3), a salt. Potassium nitrate is written in the equation as separate K^+ and NO_3^- ions because it is soluble in water. **A neutralization reaction produces water and a salt.** Some salts, such as potassium nitrate, are soluble. Others form precipitates because they are insoluble.

Figure 24 These salt flats were left behind in Death Valley, California, when the water in which the salts were dissolved evaporated.

 ## Section 3 Review

1. What ions would you expect to find when an acid dissolves in water? What ions would you expect to find when a base dissolves in water?

2. If the pH of a solution is 6, would you expect to find more or fewer hydrogen ions (H^+) than in a solution with a pH of 3? Explain why.

3. What does the term *salt* mean to a chemist, and how may a salt form?

4. **Thinking Critically Predicting** What salt would form from a reaction between hydrochloric acid, HCl, and calcium hydroxide, $Ca(OH)_2$? Explain your answer.

Check Your Progress

CHAPTER PROJECT 3

Use each indicator to test for acids and bases in familiar substances. For example, try vinegar, household ammonia, lemon juice, milk, and soapy water. (*Hint:* Use small amounts of indicator and test samples. Watch for a color change, especially where the sample comes in contact with the indicator. If you cannot see any change, add a few more drops of the sample.) Summarize your results in a table.

The Antacid Test

Consumers see or hear ads for antacids on television, radio, and in magazines. Each product claims to "neutralize excess stomach acid" best. You can experiment to see if some antacids really do work better than others.

Problem

Which antacid neutralizes more stomach acid?

Skills Focus

designing experiments, measuring, interpreting data

Materials

3 plastic droppers   small plastic cups
dilute HCl, 50 mL
methyl orange solution, 1 mL
liquid antacid, 30 mL of each brand tested

Procedure

Part 1

1. Using a plastic dropper, put 10 drops of hydrochloric acid, HCl, into one cup.
   CAUTION: *Hydrochloric acid is corrosive. Rinse spills and splashes immediately with water.*

2. Use another plastic dropper to put 10 drops of liquid antacid into another cup.

3. In your notebook, make a data table like the one below. Record the colors of the HCl and the antacid.

4. Add two drops of methyl orange solution to each cup. Record the colors you see.

5. Test each of the other antacids. Discard all the solutions and cups as directed by your teacher.

Part 2

6. Methyl orange changes color at a pH of about 4. Predict the color of the solution you expect to see when an antacid is added to a mixture of methyl orange and HCl.

7. Design a procedure for testing the reactions of each antacid with HCl. Decide how many drops of acid and methyl orange you need to use each time.

DATA TABLE

Substance	Original Color	Color With Indicator
HCl		
Antacid Brand A		
Antacid Brand B		

8. Devise a plan for adding the antacid so that you can detect when a change occurs. Decide how much antacid to add each time and how to mix the solutions in order to be sure the indicator is giving accurate results.
9. Make a second data table to record the observations you will need to make.
10. Carry out your procedure and record your results.
11. Discard the solutions and cups as directed by your teacher. Rinse the plastic droppers thoroughly.
12. Wash your hands thoroughly when done.

Analyze and Conclude

1. What is the function of the methyl orange solution?
2. Do your observations support your predictions from Step 6? Explain why or why not.
3. Why do you think antacids reduce stomach acid? Explain your answer, using the observations you made.
4. Why is it important to use the same number of drops of HCl in each trial?

5. Which antacid neutralized the HCl with the smallest number of drops? Give a possible explanation for the difference.
6. If you have the same volume (number of drops) of each antacid, which one can neutralize more acid?
7. Did your procedure give results from which you could draw conclusions? Explain why or why not. What would you do differently if you were to do the tests again?
8. **Apply** If you want to buy an antacid, what information do you need in order to compare different antacid brands?

Getting Involved

Look for antacids in a local grocery store or drug store. Check the ingredient lists of several brands. What are some of the different bases used in commercial antacids? (*Hints:* Look for compounds containing "hydroxide." Check out any compound identified as the "active ingredient.") Compare the advertised strength of several brands.

SECTION 4 Digestion and pH

DISCOVER ••••••••••••••••••••••••••••••••••••ACTIVITY••••

Where Does Digestion Begin?

1. Obtain a bite-sized piece of crusty bread.

2. Chew the bread for about one minute. Do not swallow until after you notice a change in taste as you chew.

Think It Over

Inferring How did the bread taste before and after you chewed it? How can you explain the change in taste?

GUIDE FOR READING

◆ Why is it necessary for your body to digest food?

◆ How does pH affect digestion?

Reading Tip Before you read, preview Figure 27. List the organs of the digestive system in the order in which food passes through them.

You've probably seen the following commercial: A man has a stomachache after eating spicy food. A voice announces that the problem is excess stomach acid. The remedy is an antacid tablet.

Ads like this one highlight the role of chemistry in digestion. You need to have acid in your stomach. But too much acid is a problem. Other parts of your digestive system need to be basic. What roles do acids and bases play in the digestion of food?

What Is Digestion?

Foods are made mostly of three groups of compounds: carbohydrates, proteins, and fats. But your body can't use foods in the forms you eat. **Foods must be broken down into simpler substances that your body can use for raw materials and energy.** The process of **digestion** breaks down the complex molecules of foods into smaller molecules.

Digestion involves two processes—mechanical and chemical digestion. **Mechanical digestion** tears, grinds, and mashes large food particles into smaller ones. The result is similar to hitting a sugar cube with a hammer. The size of the food is reduced, but the foods aren't changed into other compounds. **Chemical digestion** breaks large molecules into smaller molecules. Some molecules provide your body with energy. Others serve as building blocks for the compounds in muscle, bone, blood, skin, and other organs.

Figure 25 Each food molecule in this bite of a sandwich is about to begin a journey that includes changing pH.

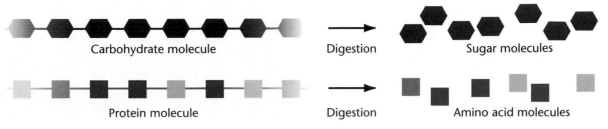

Carbohydrate molecule → Digestion → Sugar molecules

Protein molecule → Digestion → Amino acid molecules

Figure 26 Carbohydrates and proteins are large molecules that must be broken down by digestion. *Interpreting Diagrams What smaller molecules result in each case?*

Chemical digestion takes place with the help of enzymes. Enzymes are catalysts that speed up reactions in living things. Enzymes require just the right conditions to work, including temperature and pH. **For some digestive enzymes, the pH must be low. For others, the pH must be high or neutral.**

☑ *Checkpoint* What happens to foods in your body?

pH in the Digestive System

A bite of sandwich is about to take a journey through your digestive system. What pH changes will affect the food molecules along the way? Figure 27 shows the main parts of the human digestive system. As you read, trace the food's pathway through the body.

Your Mouth The first stop in the journey is your mouth. Immediately, your teeth chew and mash the food. The food also gets wet with a fluid called saliva. Have you ever felt your mouth water at the smell of something delicious? The odor of food triggers extra production of saliva.

What would you expect the ususal pH inside your mouth to be? Remember that saliva tastes neither sour nor bitter. So you're correct if you think your mouth has a pH near 7, the neutral point.

Saliva contains amylase (AM uh lays), an enzyme that helps break down the carbohydrate starch into smaller sugar molecules. Amylase works best when the pH is near 7. You can sense the action of this enzyme if you chew a piece of bread. After about two minutes in your mouth, the carbohydrate is broken into sugars. This makes the bread taste sweet.

Your Stomach Next, the food is swallowed and arrives in your stomach. This muscular organ starts digestion of foods that contain protein, such as meat, fish, and beans. Cells in the lining of your stomach release solutions that include hydrochloric acid. Rather than the near-neutral pH of your mouth, the pH drops to a very acidic level of about 2. This pH is even more acidic than the juice of a lemon.

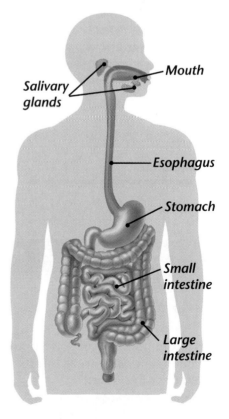

Mouth

Salivary glands

Esophagus

Stomach

Small intestine

Large intestine

Figure 27 Foods undergo changes in pH as they move through the digestive system.

Figure 28
Shrimp contains protein. Rice and pea pods contain carbohydrates.

Why does your stomach have such a low pH? The main enzyme that works in your stomach is pepsin. It helps break down proteins into small molecules called amino acids. Most enzymes work best in a solution that is nearly neutral. But pepsin is different. It works most effectively in acids.

Your Small Intestine Your stomach empties its contents into the small intestine. Here, other digestive fluids surround the food. One fluid contains the bicarbonate ion (HCO_3^-). This ion creates a slightly basic solution, so the pH in the small intestine rises to about 8. A large variety of enzymes complete the breakdown of carbohydrates, fats, and proteins. All of these enzymes work best in a slightly basic solution. Most chemical digestion ends in the small intestine.

The food molecules from the bite of sandwich have been split up into smaller ones by now. These smaller molecules are absorbed into your bloodstream and carried to the cells that will use them.

Figure 29 The pH varies greatly through the digestive system. *Relating Cause and Effect Why do certain digestive enzymes work only in certain parts of the digestive system?*

pH Changes During Digestion	
Organ	**pH**
Mouth	7
Stomach	2
Small intestine	8

Section 4 Review

1. How are foods changed by your digestive system?
2. How does pH differ in your mouth, your stomach, and your small intestine? Why are the differences important?
3. What two processes of digestion begin in the mouth? How do they differ?
4. **Thinking Critically Predicting** How would the digestion of food be affected if your stomach did not produce hydrochloric acid?

Check Your Progress
CHAPTER PROJECT 3
Use indicator paper for testing pH to find the pH of each substance you tested earlier. Add to your data table the pH value you measure for each substance. Compare the results using your indicators with the pH values you measure.

SECTION 1 — Working With Solutions

Key Ideas

◆ A solution is a well-mixed mixture. Particles dissolved in a liquid solution cannot be seen or separated by settling or filtration.

◆ In a solution, solute particles separate from each other and become surrounded by particles of the solvent.

◆ Every solute has a specific solubility in a particular solvent. Solubility changes with temperature, pressure, and type of solvent.

◆ Solutes affect the freezing points and boiling points of solvents.

Key Terms

suspension	concentrated solution
solution	solubility
solvent	saturated solution
solute	unsaturated solution
dilute solution	

SECTION 2 — Describing Acids and Bases

Key Ideas

◆ An acid tastes sour, reacts with metals and carbonates, and turns litmus red.

◆ A base tastes bitter, feels slippery, and turns litmus blue.

◆ An indicator is a substance that turns different colors in an acid or a base.

Key Terms

acid	indicator
corrosive	base

SECTION 3 — Acids and Bases in Solution

Key Ideas

◆ An acid forms hydrogen ions (H^+) when it dissolves in water.

◆ A base forms hydroxide ions (OH^-) when it dissolves in water.

◆ The pH measures the acidity of a solution. A pH value below 7 indicates an acid. A value above 7 is a base. A neutral solution has a pH of 7.

◆ When a base reacts with an acid, water and a salt form.

Key Terms

hydrogen ion (H^+)	acid rain
hydroxide ion (OH^-)	neutralization
pH scale	salt

SECTION 4 — Digestion and pH

INTEGRATING LIFE SCIENCE

Key Ideas

◆ Digestion breaks down complex foods into simpler materials that can be used for energy and raw materials by the body.

◆ Enzymes in the digestive system do not all work best at the same pH. The pH values vary from the mouth, to the stomach, to the small intestine.

Key Terms

digestion	chemical digestion
mechanical digestion	

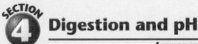

USING THE INTERNET

www.science-explorer.phschool.com

ACTIVITY

Reviewing Content

For more review of key concepts, see the
Interactive Student Tutorial CD-ROM.

Multiple Choice
Choose the letter of the best answer.

1. Sugar water is an example of a
   a. suspension.   b. solution.
   c. solute.   d. solvent.
2. A solution in which as much solute as
   possible is dissolved in a solvent is a
   a. dilute solution.
   b. filtered solution.
   c. saturated solution.
   d. unsaturated solution.
3. Washing soda (Na_2CO_3) will make
   bubbles if you add
   a. tap water.   b. salt water.
   c. ammonia cleaner. d. lemon juice.
4. Litmus and cabbage juice are examples of
   a. indicators.
   b. strong acids.
   c. strong bases.
   d. concentrated solutions.
5. If a base separates completely into ions
   when dissolved in water, it is a
   a. weak acid.
   b. weak base.
   c. strong acid.
   d. strong base.

True or False
*If the statement is true, write true. If it is false,
change the underlined word or words to make the
statement true.*

6. The solubility of a gas in water goes up if
   you <u>increase</u> the temperature.
7. The slightly sour taste of lemonade tells
   you that it is a <u>base</u>.
8. The gas produced when an acid reacts
   with a carbonate is <u>oxygen</u>.
9. Dilute hydrochloric acid is an example of
   a <u>strong</u> acid.
10. Amylase, the enzyme in saliva that helps
    to break down carbohydrates into simple
    sugars, works best in a <u>neutral</u> solution.

Checking Concepts

11. Describe at least two differences between
    a dilute solution and a concentrated
    solution of sugar water.
12. You have three different unknown com-
    pounds that are all white powders. How
    can you use solubility to identify each
    compound?
13. Tomatoes are acidic. Predict two
    properties of tomato juice that you would
    be able to observe.
14. Explain how an indicator helps you
    distinguish between an acid and a base.
15. What combination of acid and base can
    be used to make the salt potassium
    chloride, KCl?
16. **Writing to Learn** Some of the
    limestone on the outside of buildings in
    an area looks as if it is being gradually
    eaten away. As an investigator for the
    local air pollution agency, write a brief
    memo explaining what may be causing
    the problem.

Thinking Visually

17. **Concept Map** Copy the concept map
    about solutions onto a separate sheet of
    paper. Then complete it and add a title.
    (For more on concept maps, see the Skills
    Handbook.)

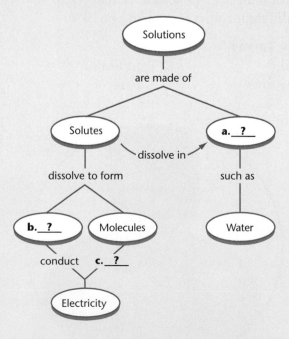

Applying Skills

The diagram below shows the particles of an unknown acid in a water solution. Use the diagram to answer Questions 18–20.

Water

Acid

18. **Interpreting Data** How can you tell from the diagram that the acid is weak?
19. **Making Models** Suppose another unknown acid is a strong acid. Make a diagram to show the particles of this acid dissolved in water.
20. **Drawing Conclusions** Explain how the pH of a strong acid compares with the pH of a weak acid of the same concentration.

Thinking Critically

21. **Developing Hypotheses** Some power plants release hot wastewater into nearby rivers or streams. Fish living in these waters sometimes die from lack of oxygen. Write a hypothesis to explain what has happened to the oxygen in the water.
22. **Comparing and Contrasting** Compare the types of particles formed in a water solution of an acid with those formed in a water solution of a base.
23. **Applying Concepts** When calcium oxide (CaO) dissolves in water, it reacts as shown below. Is calcium oxide an acid or a base? Explain.

$$CaO + H_2O \rightarrow Ca^{2+} + 2OH^-$$

24. **Predicting** Predict what type of food might not be digested well if someone took greater than the recommended dose of antacid tablets. Explain.

Performance Assessment

CHAPTER PROJECT 3 Wrap Up

Present Your Project Demonstrate the indicators you tested. Make a list of the substances you tested in order from most acidic to least acidic.

Reflect and Record In your journal, discuss whether or not you would use the same materials as indicators if you did this project again. Explain why. Describe how acid-base indicators could be useful for farmers and gardeners. Would you recommend that they use any of the indicators you made?

Getting Involved

In Your Community Find out the acidity of rainfall in your area. Collect a small sample of rainwater, if possible, and test its pH. How does it compare to the pH of normal rainwater? If you tested rain at different times of the year, do you think the pH would differ? Design an experiment to demonstrate how you would test the pH in your community at different times.

Exploring Materials

PROJECT 4

Polymer Profiles

A spider's delicate web glistens in the early morning sunshine. It was spun overnight from silken fibers produced by the spider's body. These fibers, much of the spider itself, and the flower stems that support the web are made from polymers—one of the types of materials you will study in this chapter. In your project, you will survey different polymers found around you. You will learn about the properties of these materials and see how their uses depend on their properties.

Your Goal To collect and investigate different polymers.

To complete your project you must
◆ collect at least eight polymer samples from at least three different locations
◆ investigate the chemical and physical properties of the polymers by performing at least three tests
◆ create an informative display about these polymers
◆ follow the safety guidelines in Appendix A

Get Started Brainstorm with your classmates what you already know about polymers. Make a list of items you think are made of polymers. Look in Section 1 to get some hints about materials to investigate. Begin to think about how different polymers are used in everyday life, and why.

Check Your Progress You will be working on this project as you study this chapter. To keep your project on track, look for Check Your Progress boxes at the following points.

Section 1 Review, page 119: Collect samples of polymers and record data about their sources and uses.

Section 3 Review, page 132: Devise procedures to test properties of the polymers.

Section 4 Review, page 139: Carry out your tests and organize your results in your data table.

Wrap Up At the end of the chapter (page 143), you will present a showcase of polymers to the class.

SECTION 4 **Radioactive Elements**

Discover **How Much Goes Away?**
Sharpen Your Skills **Predicting**
Sharpen Your Skills **Calculating**
Skills Lab **That's Half-Life!**

This spider's web and the mountain thistle stems that support it are made of natural polymers.

SECTION
① Polymers and Composites

DISCOVER ••••••••••••••••••••••••••••••••••••••• ACTIVITY

What Did You Make?

1. 🥽 Look at a sample of borax solution and write down properties you observe. Do the same with white glue.

2. Measure about 2 tablespoons of borax solution into a paper cup.

3. Stir the solution as you add about a tablespoon of white glue to the cup.

4. After 2 minutes, record the properties of the material in the cup. Wash your hands when you are finished.

Think It Over

Observing What evidence of a chemical reaction did you observe? How did the materials change? What do you think you made?

GUIDE FOR READING

◆ How does a polymer form?

◆ Why are composite materials often more useful than single polymers?

Reading Tip As you read, make a list of properties of polymers. Write one sentence describing each property.

Did you ever step into tar on a hot summer day? Tar is a thick, smelly, black goo that sticks to your shoes. Tar, from crude oil or coal, can be made into rope, insulating fabric for clothes, and safety gear. Manufacturers use tar to make countless products ranging from sports equipment and automobile parts to plastic housewares and toys.

Look around the room. How many things can you see that are made of plastic? What materials do you think people used to make these items before plastic was invented? Many things that were once made of metal, glass, paper, or wood have been replaced by plastic materials.

Figure 1 The clothing, boots, goggles, and helmet worn by this climber are all made of polymers. So is the rope that protects her from falling off this frozen waterfall in Colorado.

Carbon's Strings, Rings, and Other Things

Plastics and the cells in your body have something in common. They are made of carbon compounds. Carbon compounds contain atoms of carbon bonded to each other and to other kinds of atoms. Carbon is present in more than two million known compounds, and more are being discovered or invented every day.

Carbon's unique ability to form so many compounds comes from two properties. Carbon atoms can form four covalent bonds. They can also bond to each other in chains and ring-shaped groups. These structures form the "backbones" to which other atoms attach.

Hydrogen is the most common element found with carbon in its compounds. Other elements include oxygen, nitrogen, phosphorus, sulfur, and the halogens, especially chlorine.

Carbon Compounds Form Polymers

Molecules of some carbon compounds can hook together, forming larger molecules. A **polymer** (PAHL uh mur) is a large, complex molecule built from smaller molecules joined together. The smaller molecules from which polymers are built are called **monomers** (MAHN uh murz). **Polymers form when chemical bonds link large numbers of monomers in a repeating pattern.** A polymer may consist of hundreds or even thousands of monomers.

Many polymers consist of a single kind of monomer that repeats over and over again. You could think of these monomers as linked like the identical cars of a long passenger train. In other cases, two or three monomers may join in an alternating pattern. Sometimes links between monomer chains occur, forming large webs or netlike molecules. The chemical properties of a polymer depend on the monomers from which it is made.

☑ *Checkpoint* *What are the patterns in which monomers come together to form polymers?*

Figure 2 Carbon atoms can form straight chains, branched chains, and rings. In these drawings, lines represent covalent bonds that can form between atoms. *Interpreting Diagrams How many covalent bonds does each carbon atom form?*

Building a Polymer

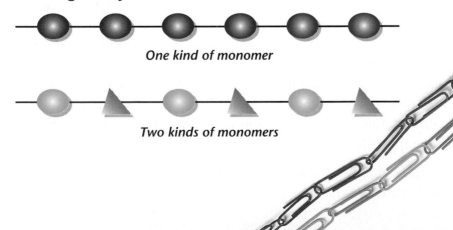

One kind of monomer

Two kinds of monomers

Figure 3 Like chains of paper clips made of the same or different pieces, polymers can be built from one kind or several kinds of monomers.

Figure 4 Both animals and plants make polymers. **A.** The leaves and stems of these desert plants are made of cellulose and other polymers. **B.** A cotton plant is a source of polymers that people make into thread and cloth. **C.** These silk fabrics were made from the threads of silkworm cocoons. *Comparing and Contrasting What do the polymers shown in these photos have in common?*

Natural Polymers

INTEGRATING LIFE SCIENCE Polymers have been around as long as life on Earth. Plants, animals, and other living things produce many natural materials made of large polymer molecules.

Plant Polymers Look closely at a piece of coarse paper, such as a paper towel. You can see that it is made of long strings, or fibers. These fibers are bundles of cellulose. **Cellulose** (SEL yoo lohs) is a flexible but strong natural polymer that gives shape to plant cells. Cellulose is made in plants when sugar molecules (made earlier from carbon dioxide and water) are joined into long strands. The cellulose then forms cell structures.

Animal Polymers Gently touch a spider web and feel how it stretches without breaking. It is made from chemicals in the spider's body. These chemicals mix and react to form a silken polymer that is one of the strongest materials known. Spiders spin webs, egg cases, and traps for prey from these fibers. You can wear polymers made by animals. Silk is made from the fibers of silkworm cocoons. Wool is made from sheep's fur. These polymers can be woven into thread and cloth.

Your own body makes polymers. Tap your fingernail on a tabletop. Your fingernails and the muscles that just moved your finger are made of proteins. Proteins are polymers. Within your body, proteins are assembled from combinations of smaller molecules (monomers), called amino acids. The properties of a protein depend on which amino acids are used and in what order. One combination builds the protein that forms your fingernails. Another combination forms the protein that carries oxygen in your blood. Yet another forms the hair that grows on your head.

Checkpoint *What are two examples of natural polymers from plants and animals?*

Synthetic Polymers

Many polymers you use every day are synthesized from simpler materials. Recall that a synthesis reaction occurs when elements or simple compounds combine to form complex compounds. The starting materials for polymers come from coal or oil. **Plastics,** which are synthetic polymers that can be molded or shaped, are the most common products. But there are many others. Carpets, clothing, glue, and even chewing gum can be made of synthetic polymers.

Figure 5 lists just a few of the hundreds of polymers people use. Although the names seem like tongue-twisters, see how many you recognize. You may be able to identify some polymers by their initials printed on the bottoms of plastic bottles.

Compare the uses of polymers listed in Figure 5 with their characteristics. Notice that many products require materials that are flexible, yet strong. Others must be hard or lightweight. When chemical engineers design a new product, they have to think about how it will be used. Then they synthesize a polymer with properties to match.

Synthetic polymers are often used in place of natural materials that are too expensive or wear out too quickly. Polyester and nylon fabrics, for example, are used instead of wool, silk, and cotton to make clothes. Laminated countertops and vinyl floors replace wood in many kitchens. Other synthetic polymers have uses for which there is no suitable natural material. Compact discs, computer parts, artificial heart valves, and even your bicycle tires couldn't exist without synthetic polymers.

Language Arts
CONNECTION

Many words in the English language use prefixes from Greek or Latin. In Greek, *mono-* means "one" and *poly-* means "many." These prefixes tell you that the molecules are made of either one or many parts.

In Your Journal

Make a list of words with other prefixes that tell you "how many," for example, the *tri-* in triangle. Tell what number the prefix indicates. Extend your list to include units of measurement, such as the millimeter. In each case, tell what information the prefix gives.

Figure 5 You can find many applications of synthetic polymers in your own home.

Some Synthetic Polymers You Use		
Name	**Characteristics**	**Uses**
Low-density polyethylene (LDPE)	Flexible, soft, melts easily	Plastic bags, squeeze bottles, electric wire insulation
High-density polyethylene (HDPE)	Stronger than LDPE; higher melting temperatures	Detergent bottles, gas cans, toys, milk jugs
Polypropylene (PP)	Hard, keeps its shape	Toys, car parts, bottle caps
Polyvinyl chloride (PVC)	Tough, flexible	Garden hoses, imitation leather, piping
Polystyrene (PS)	Lightweight, can be made into foam	Foam drinking cups, insulation, furniture, "peanut" packing material
Nylon	Strong, can be drawn into flexible thread	Stockings, parachutes, fishing line, fabric
Teflon (polytetrafluoroethylene)	Nonreactive, low friction	Nonstick coating for cooking pans

Composites

Every substance has its advantages and disadvantages. What would happen if you could take the best properties of two substances and put them together? **Composites** combine two or more substances as a new material with different properties. **By combining the useful properties of two or more substances in a composite, chemists can make a new material that works better than either one alone.** Many composite materials include one or more polymers.

SCIENCE & History

The Development of Polymers

The first synthetic polymers were made by changing natural polymers in some way. Later, crude oil and coal became the starting materials. Now new polymers are designed in laboratories every year.

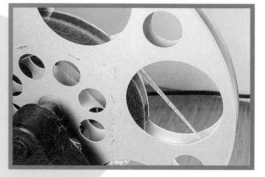

1869 Celluloid

Made using cellulose, celluloid became a substitute for ivory in billiard balls and combs and brushes. It was later used to make movie film. Because celluloid is very flammable, other materials have replaced it for almost all purposes, except table-tennis balls.

1825   **1875**

1839 Synthetic Rubber

Charles Goodyear invented a process that turned natural rubber into a hard, stretchable polymer. It did not get sticky and soft when heated or become brittle when cold, as natural rubber does. Bicycle tires were an early use.

1909 Bakelite

Bakelite was the first commercial polymer made from compounds in coal tar. Bakelite doesn't get soft when heated, and it doesn't conduct electricity. These properties made it useful for handles for pots and pans, telephones, and for parts in electrical outlets.

A Natural Composite The idea of putting two different materials together to get the advantages of both comes from the natural world. Many synthetic composites are designed to imitate a common natural composite—wood. Wood is made of long fibers of cellulose, held together by another plant polymer called lignin. Cellulose fibers are flexible and can't support much weight. At the same time, lignin is brittle and would crack under the weight of the tree branches. But the combination of the two polymers makes a strong tree trunk.

In Your Journal

Find out more about the invention of one of these polymers. Write a headline for a newspaper, announcing the invention. Then write the first paragraph of the news article telling how the invention will change people's lives.

1989 LEP

Light-emitting polymers (LEP) are plastics that give off light when exposed to low-voltage electricity. Research on LEPs points toward their use as flexible and more easy-to-read viewing screens in computers, digital camera monitors, watch-size phones, and televisions.

1934 Nylon

A giant breakthrough came with a synthetic fiber that imitates silk. Nylon replaced expensive silk in women's stockings and fabric for parachutes and clothing. It can also be molded to make objects like buttons, gears, and zippers.

1925 — **1975** — **2025**

1952 Fiberglass Composite

Fiberglass is mixed with polymers to form a material with the strength of glass fibers and the moldability of plastic. Fiberglass composite is useful for boat and airplane parts because it is much lighter than metal, and it doesn't rust.

1971 Kevlar

Kevlar is five times as strong as the same weight of steel. This polymer is tough enough to substitute for steel ropes and cables in offshore oil-drilling rigs, but light enough to use as parts for spacecraft. Kevlar is also used in protective clothing for firefighters and police officers.

Figure 6 Fiberglass makes a snowboard (left) both lightweight and strong. The composites in a fishing rod (right) make it so flexible that it will not break when pulling in a large fish.

Synthetic Composites The idea of combining the properties of two substances to make a more useful one has led to many new products. Fiberglass composites are one example. Strands of glass fiber are woven together and strengthened with a liquid plastic that sets like glue. The combination makes a strong, hard solid that may be molded around a form to give it shape. These composites are lightweight, but strong enough to be used as a boat hull or car body. Fiberglass also resists corrosion. It will not rust as metal does.

Other composites made from strong polymers combined with lightweight ones have many uses. Bicycles, automobiles, and airplanes built from such composites are much lighter than the same vehicles built from steel or aluminum. Some composites are used to make fishing rods, tennis racquets, and other sports equipment that need to be flexible but strong.

Too Many Polymers?

INTEGRATING ENVIRONMENTAL SCIENCE It is difficult to look around without seeing something made of synthetic polymers. They have replaced many natural materials for several reasons. First, polymers are inexpensive to make. Second, they are strong. Finally, they last a long time.

But synthetic polymers have caused some problems, too. Many of the disadvantages of using plastics come from the same properties that make them so useful. It is often cheaper to throw away plastic materials and make new ones than it is to reuse them. As a result, they increase the volume of trash. Most plastics don't

Sharpen your Skills

Classifying ACTIVITY

Sit or stand where you have a clear view of the room you are in. Slowly sweep the room with your eyes, making a list of the objects you see. Do the same sweep of the clothes you are wearing. Check off those items on your list made (completely or partly) of natural or synthetic polymers. What percent of the items were *not* made with polymers?

react very easily with other chemical compounds. This means they don't break down into simpler materials in the environment. In contrast, natural polymers do. Some plastics are expected to last thousands of years. How do you get rid of something that lasts that long?

Is there a way to solve these problems? One solution is to use waste plastics as raw material for making new plastic products. You know this idea as recycling. Recycling has led to industries that create new products from discarded plastics. Bottles, fabrics for clothing, and parts for new cars are just some of the many items that can come from waste plastics. A pile of empty soda bottles can even be turned into synthetic wood. Look around your neighborhood, and you may see park benches or "wooden" fences made from recycled plastics. Through recycling, the disposal problem is solved and new, useful items are created.

Figure 7 These rulers are just one product made from recycled plastic bottles.
Drawing Conclusions What would have happened to these bottles if they weren't recycled?

Section 1 Review

1. How are monomers related to polymers?
2. What advantage does a composite have over the individual materials from which it is made?
3. Why is it possible for carbon to form so many different kinds of compounds?
4. Make a list of polymers you can find in your home. Classify them as natural or synthetic.
5. **Thinking Critically Making Judgments** Think of something plastic that you have used today. Is there some other material that would be better than plastic for this use?

Check Your Progress

CHAPTER PROJECT 4

Collect a variety of different polymers. You might look in tool chests, kitchen cabinets, closets or drawers, art classrooms, hardware stores, or outdoors. Be sure to record where you found the polymer and what its function is. Record any information on labels or packaging. Try to identify each polymer as natural or synthetic. Organize this information into a list.

You, the Consumer

Packaging With Polymers

You need to mail some breakable items to a friend in another state. There are a variety of different polymer materials that you could use to package these items for mailing. In this lab, you will design an experiment to find out more about these materials. Then you will decide which one you would use.

Problem

Which polymer material or combination of materials should you choose for packaging?

Skills Focus

designing experiments, controlling variables, drawing conclusions

Suggested Materials

water   hand lens   weights (or books)
scissors   tape   thermometers
balance   clock or timer
containers (beakers, trays, plastic cups)
iodine solution, 1% solution
hard-boiled eggs (optional)
polymers used in packaging (paper, Tyvek,
    plastic foam, ecofoam, cardboard, fabric,
    popcorn, sawdust, wood shavings, or plastic)

Procedure

1. Write a hypothesis about the ideal properties a polymer should have if it is to be used for packaging.
2. Make a list of all the ways you can think of to test the properties of polymers. Think about properties including, but not limited to, the following:
   - ability to protect a fragile object
   - reaction to water   - appearance
   - heat insulation   - strength
   - reaction to iodine   - mass

   (*Note:* Iodine turns a dark blue-black color when starch is present. Starch may attract insects or other pests.)

DATA TABLE

	Brief Description of Test 1	Brief Description of Test 2	Brief Description of Test 3	Brief Description of Test 4
Polymer A				
Polymer B				
Polymer C				

3. Select a property you wish to test. Choose a method that you think would be the best way to test that property.
4. Design a step-by-step procedure for the test. Do the same for each of the other properties you decide to investigate. Be sure that you change only one variable at a time. Include any safety directions in your procedure.
5. Predict which polymers you think will perform best in each test you plan.
6. After your teacher has approved your procedure, perform the tests on a sample of each polymer.
7. Record your observations in a table similar to the one on the left.

Analyze and Conclude

1. Describe the similarities and differences that you discovered among your samples.
2. Review the different tests that you used. Which worked well? Are there any tests you would do differently if you were to do them another time?

3. Which polymer, or polymers, would you use to package your items for mailing? Explain your reasons for this choice.
4. Which polymer, or polymers, would you not want to use? Why?
5. **Apply** Tyvek costs more than paper. Ecofoam costs more than plastic foam. How would this information influence your decision on which material to use?

Design an Experiment

A vending machine must be able to drop a cookie a distance of 1.5 m without breaking it. Design an experiment to determine how you could make a package that is strong, cheap, and environmentally friendly. With your teacher's approval, perform the experiment.

Grocery Bags: Paper or Plastic?

Americans use more than 32 billion grocery bags each year. About 80 percent of the bags are plastic. The other 20 percent are paper. Plastic bags are made from crude oil, a resource that cannot be replaced. Paper bags, on the other hand, are made from trees. Trees are a renewable resource, but it takes time to grow them.

Both paper and plastic grocery bags end up in the trash. Although some bags are incinerated, or burned, most end up buried in landfills. You need a way to carry groceries home. Which bag should you choose at the grocery store— paper or plastic?

The Issues

Should People Choose Paper Bags?
Paper bags can hold more items than plastic. A typical paper bag can hold about 12 items. A plastic bag might hold half as many.

A mature tree can yield about 700 bags. But just one large supermarket can use 700 bags in less than an hour! Most trees that are used to make paper come from forests. Only about 20 percent come from tree farms.

Hazardous chemicals are used in making paper bags. Wood and certain poisonous chemical compounds are heated. The mixture is cooked into a mush of wood fibers, which is pressed into paper.

Usually, paper bags are biodegradable, which means that decay organisms break them down. But in tightly packed landfills, even paper bags don't break down easily.

Should People Choose Plastic Bags?
Plastic bags are lightweight, compact, and waterproof. They take up 80 percent less space in landfills than an equal number of paper bags. But most plastic bags are not biodegradable. They cannot be broken down by natural processes. They can last a long time in landfills.

Some plastic bags end up in the ocean. There they are a danger to sea birds and animals who may eat or get caught in them.

Plastic bags are made from a compound that's left over when crude oil is made into fuel. This waste product used to be discarded or burned.

Most plastic can be recycled. Unfortunately, only about 10 percent of all plastic products are recycled today. Most people are just not recycling.

Which Is the Right Choice?
Some people want laws that would require manufacturers to make all bags—paper and plastic—out of recycled materials. Paper manufacturers say, however, that the fibers in recycled paper are too short to make bags that are strong enough.

The right choice of bags may depend on how your community handles trash. Does it collect paper or plastic or both to be recycled?

Both paper and plastic bags can be reused in many ways, such as for storage or trash containers liners. But the best choice may be neither paper nor plastic. One reusable cloth bag could replace hundreds of paper and plastic bags.

You Decide

1. Identify the Problem
In your own words, explain the problems in choosing paper or plastic bags.

2. Analyze the Options
List the pros and cons of using plastic and paper bags. In each case, who will benefit? Who might be harmed?

3. Find a Solution
Your community wants to pass a law to regulate the kind of grocery bags that stores should offer. Take a stand. Defend your position.

SECTION 2 Metals and Alloys

DISCOVER ·· ACTIVITY

Are They Steel the Same?

1. Wrap a cut nail (low-carbon steel), a wire nail (high-carbon steel) and a stainless steel bolt together in a paper towel.

2. Place the towel in a plastic bag. Add about a cup of salt water and seal the bag.

3. After one or two days, remove the nails and bolt. Note any changes in the metals.

Think It Over

Developing Hypotheses What happened to the three types of steel? Which one changed the most, and which changed the least? What do you think accounts for the difference?

O ver 6,000 years ago, people learned to make copper knives and tools that were sharper than stone tools. Later, they discovered that they could also use tin for tools. But these metals are soft, so they bend easily and are hard to keep sharp. About 5,000 years ago, metal makers discovered a way to make better tools. Copper and tin mixed together in the right amounts make a stronger, harder metal that keeps its sharp edge after long use. This discovery was the beginning of the Bronze Age. It also was the invention of the first alloy. An **alloy** is a substance made of two or more elements that has the properties of metal. In every alloy, at least one of the elements is a metal.

GUIDE FOR READING

◆ What properties make alloys useful?

Reading Tip Before you read, rewrite the headings in the section as *how, why,* or *what* questions. As you read, look for answers to these questions.

Properties of Metals

You know a piece of metal when you see it. It's hard and usually shiny. At room temperature all metallic elements (except mercury) are solids. Metals share other properties, too. They can conduct electricity. They also can be drawn out into thin wire. Copper, for example, made into wire, is used to carry electric current to the outlets in your home. Metals can be hammered into a sheet. Aluminum, rolled flat, makes aluminum foil. You wouldn't be able to try that with a piece of glass!

Gold leaf dome of City Hall in Savannah, Georgia ▶

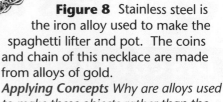

Figure 8 Stainless steel is the iron alloy used to make the spaghetti lifter and pot. The coins and chain of this necklace are made from alloys of gold.
Applying Concepts Why are alloys used to make these objects rather than the pure metals?

Properties of Alloys

The properties of an alloy can differ greatly from those of its individual elements. Bronze, for example, is an alloy of copper and tin. It was a much better material for early toolmaking because it was harder than either element alone.

Pure gold is soft and easily bent. Gold jewelry and coins are made of an alloy of gold with another metal, such as copper or silver. These gold alloys are much harder than pure gold but still let its beauty show. Even after thousands of years, objects made of gold alloys still look exactly the same as when they were first made.

Alloys are used much more than pure metals because they are generally stronger and less likely to react with air or water. You have seen iron objects rust when they are exposed to air and water. But forks and spoons made of stainless steel can be washed over and over again without rusting. Stainless steel is an alloy of iron, carbon, nickel, and chromium. It does not react as easily with air and water as iron does. *Exploring Alloys and Metals in Aircraft* shows how other properties of alloys may be put to use.

☑ *Checkpoint* Why is bronze more useful for tools than copper or tin?

Making Alloys

Many alloys are made by melting metals and mixing them together in carefully measured amounts. Since the beginning of the Bronze Age, this technique has been used to make copper alloys. Some modern alloys are made by mixing the elements as powders and then heating them under high pressure. This process uses less energy because the metals blend at lower temperatures. The material then can be molded into the desired shape immediately. Another recent technique, called ion implantation, involves firing a beam of ions at a metal. A thin layer of alloy then forms on the metal's surface. Titanium, for example, may be bombarded with nitrogen ions to make a strong alloy for artificial bone and joint replacements.

EXPLORING Alloys and Metals in Aircraft

Much of the structure of an aircraft is made of metals. Engineers often design alloys with specific characteristics to fit the needs of the different parts of the aircraft.

Gold
A thin layer of pure gold coats the polymer (plastic) windshield. An electric current through the gold provides enough heat to keep the windshield frost-free. Gold works well for this purpose because it does not react with air and water.

Iron Alloys
The structural supports that hold the airplane together must be extremely strong. Steel made of iron with carbon and other metals is the best choice for these parts.

Aluminum Alloys
The outside of the plane has to be strong, light, and resistant to corrosion. The airplane's "skin" is aluminum, which is alloyed with magnesium, copper, and traces of other metals to increase strength.

Titanium Alloys
Landing gear must be strong enough to hold the wheels of the airplane and support its great mass. Alloys of titanium with vanadium, iron, and aluminum are strong as steel but much lighter in weight.

Nickel Alloys
The turbine blades in the jet engines have to spin around thousands of times per minute without changing shape. They also must withstand temperatures up to 1,100°C. Nickel alloyed with iron, carbon, and cobalt does the job.

Common Alloys

Alloy	Elements	Properties	Uses
Brass	Copper, zinc	Strong, resists corrosion, polishes well	Musical instruments, faucets, decorative hardware, jewelry
Bronze	Copper, tin	Hard, resists corrosion	Marine hardware, screws, grillwork
Stainless steel	Iron, carbon, nickel, chromium	Strong, resists corrosion	Tableware, cookware, surgical instruments
Carbon steel	Iron, carbon	Inexpensive, strong	Tools, auto bodies, machinery, steel girders, rails
Plumber's solder	Lead, tin	Low melting point	Seal joints and leaks in metal plumbing
Sterling silver	Silver, copper	Shiny, harder than pure silver	Jewelry, tableware
Dental amalgam	Mercury, silver, tin, copper, zinc	Low melting point, easily shaped	Dental fillings
Pewter	Tin, antimony, copper*	Bright or satin finish, resists tarnish	Tableware, decorative objects
Wood's metal	Bismuth, lead, tin, cadmium	Low melting point	Fire sprinklers, electric fuses

*Pewter containing lead cannot be used with food.

Figure 9 Alloys have a wide variety of uses.
Making Generalizations How do the properties of each alloy make it well-suited for its uses?

Using Alloys

When you want to describe something very hard or tough, you may use the expression "hard as steel." Steel is an alloy of iron with other elements. It is used for its strength, hardness, and resistance to corrosion. Without steel, suspension bridges, sky-scrapers, and surgical knives would not exist. Neither would artificial joints that replace damaged knees and hips.

Steels Not all steel is alike. Its properties depend on which elements are added to iron. High-carbon steel, for example, consists of about 0.5 percent manganese and up to 0.8 percent carbon. Carbon steel is stronger and harder than wrought iron, which is almost pure iron. Tools, knives, machinery, and appliances are just some of the uses for carbon steel. Steels with less than 0.8 percent carbon are more ductile and malleable. They may be used for nails, cables, and chains.

There are hundreds of different types of steel. Usually carbon is added to the iron plus one or more of the following metals: chromium, manganese, molybdenum, nickel, tungsten, and vanadium. Steel made with these metals is generally stronger and harder than carbon steel, and usually more corrosion-resistant. Depending on their properties, these steels may become bicycle frames, train rails, steel tubing, and construction equipment.

Figure 10 A plumber (left) takes advantage of the low melting point of the alloy solder to seal a leaking pipe. The brass in this doorknocker (below) is an alloy of copper and zinc.

Other Alloys Bronze, brass, and solder (SAHD ur) are just a few examples of other kinds of alloys. These materials are used to make items ranging from plumbing materials and sprinkler systems to tableware and doorknobs. Even your dentist uses alloys. Have you ever had a cavity in a tooth? A mixture of mercury with silver or gold (called an amalgam) makes a pasty solid. It rapidly hardens, filling a hole in the tooth. Look at Figure 9 and see how many of the examples listed in the table are alloys you have seen or used.

Section 2 Review

1. Name two properties of alloys that make them more useful than pure metals.
2. Describe one way in which alloys are made.
3. What advantage does stainless steel cookware have over cookware made of iron?
4. **Thinking Critically Applying Concepts** What properties would you look for to find out if an object was made of metal?
5. **Thinking Critically Problem Solving** The purity of gold is expressed in units called karats. A piece of 24-karat gold is pure gold metal. A piece of 12-karat gold is one half gold and one half another metal, often silver or copper. What fraction of the metal in a piece of 18-karat gold jewelry is actually gold?

Science at Home

Find items in your home that are made from metals or alloys. Look for cooking utensils, tools, toys, sports equipment, appliances, and other household items that are made with these materials. Discuss with members of your family how properties of the metals or alloys relate to the uses of the objects.

DISCOVER .... **ACTIVITY**

Does It Get Wet?

1. Find the masses of a glazed pottery flowerpot and an unglazed one of similar size. Record both values.

2. Place both pots in a basin of water for ten minutes.

3. Remove the pots from the water and blot dry gently with paper towels.

4. Find and record the masses of both flowerpots again.

5. Calculate the percent of change in mass for each pot.

Think It Over

Inferring Which pot gained the most mass? What can you infer about the effect that glazing has on the pot?

GUIDE FOR READING

◆ What properties of ceramics make them useful?

◆ How may glass be changed to make it useful?

Reading Tip Before you read, make a list of ceramic or glass items you use. As you read, look for reasons why these materials are well suited for their uses.

Picture yourself on a warm day, walking through a slow-flowing stream. The mud at the bottom is soft. It squishes up between your toes. When you pick it up and shape it with your hands, it holds its form. If you let it dry in the sun, it becomes hard. This material is clay. You could also shape the clay into blocks, add some straw to make a composite material, and let the blocks dry. If you live where there is not much rain, you could use the blocks to build a house. In fact, people have used this type of brick to build sturdy homes. The Pueblo homes of the Southwest, for example, were built this way over a thousand years ago. Some of them are still standing today.

Making Ceramics

A discovery made thousands of years ago increased the usefulness of dried clay objects. Heating clay to about 1,000°C makes it harder and stronger. **Ceramics** are hard, crystalline solids made by heating clay and other mineral materials to high temperatures. Clay is made of very small mineral particles containing silicon, aluminum, and oxygen. Other elements, such as magnesium and iron may be present in clay, too. Clay forms when the minerals in

◀ **Pueblo homes in Taos, New Mexico**

rock are broken down. Unheated clay also contains water. When a clay object is heated, much of the water present on its surface evaporates, and the particles of clay stick together.

This process forms the hard ceramic pottery used for bricks and flowerpots. Once cooled, these materials have tiny spaces in their structure that absorb and hold water. If you grow a plant in this kind of pot, you can feel the moisture in the outer surface of the clay after you water the plant. When pottery is brushed with a layer of silicon dioxide and heated again, a glassy coating, called a glaze, forms. This glaze is shiny and waterproof. You might see glazed pottery used to serve or store food. Potters often use colorful glazes to create artistic designs on their work.

☑ *Checkpoint* *How does a glaze change the properties of a ceramic?*

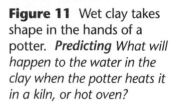

Figure 11 Wet clay takes shape in the hands of a potter. *Predicting What will happen to the water in the clay when the potter heats it in a kiln, or hot oven?*

Properties and Uses of Ceramics

Have you ever heard the phrase "a bull in a china shop"? Imagine the damage. A bull in a bronze shop just wouldn't be as dramatic! The phrase comes from the fact that ceramics are brittle and can shatter when struck. Despite their tendency to break, ceramics have several properties that make them useful. **Ceramics resist moisture, do not conduct electricity, and can withstand temperatures higher than molten metals.**

Ceramic pottery has been used for thousands of years to store food, protecting it from moisture and animals. Roofing tiles, bricks, and sewer pipes all are long-standing uses of ceramics. Ceramics also are used as insulators in electric equipment and light fixtures.

Figure 12 Some ceramics, such as these roof tiles (left), have practical uses. Other ceramics (right) are valued for their delicate beauty.

New uses for ceramics continue to be developed. The walls of ovens for making steel and other metal products are made of a type of brick that does not melt at the temperature of red-hot iron. And ceramic tiles are the only materials that can withstand the temperatures of over 1,600°C that build up on the bottom of the space shuttle during its reentry into the atmosphere. These tiles insulate the shuttle and protect the astronauts.

Figure 13 Before the space shuttle *Columbia* can be launched again, tiles damaged during its last reentry must be replaced. *Predicting* What would happen to the spacecraft if many of the tiles were missing?

✓ *Checkpoint* *What are some uses of ceramics?*

Making Glass

Have you ever looked closely at a handful of sand, or watched the varied grains as they slipped through your fingers? Thousands of years ago people learned that sand mixed with limestone can be melted into a thick, hot liquid. Most sand consists of tiny, hard pieces of quartz, a mineral made of silicon dioxide. When sand is heated to about 1,600°C, it flows like thick molasses. If this liquid cools quickly, it forms a clear, solid material with no crystal structure called **glass.**

The first glass objects were formed on clay molds that were chipped away after the glass hardened. Then about 2,000 years ago, glassmakers in ancient Persia invented glassblowing. The

Figure 14 Glass objects made in ancient Rome are on display at the Corning Museum in Corning, New York.

Figure 15 The lenses in this microscope are made from lead oxide glass. *Applying Concepts* How do the microscope lenses help this girl view a small object?

glassmaker put a blob of melted glass on the end of an iron pipe. By blowing air through the pipe, the glassmaker could produce a hollow glass vessel. If the glass was blown inside a wooden mold, jars and vases in beautiful patterns and shapes could be created.

Different materials may be added to glass to make it useful for particular purposes. Early glassmakers added calcium (as limestone) and sodium (as sodium carbonate) to the melting sand. This mixture melts at a lower temperature than sand alone, so it is easier to work with. Window glass and the bottles and jars you use every day are still made with this type of glass.

Substituting lead oxide for the limestone makes a glass that bends light in useful ways. This kind of glass is used to make lenses for eyeglasses, telescopes, and microscopes. Adding boron oxide creates a glass that resists heat better than ordinary glass. It is used for cookware and laboratory glassware that must be heated. Colored glass is made by adding minerals containing various metals to the molten glass. Selenium and gold produce red glass. Cobalt makes beautiful, deep blue glass.

Communication Through Glass

INTEGRATING PHYSICS There's a good chance that the next time you make a phone call, your message will travel through glass. An **optical fiber** is a threadlike piece of glass that can be used for transmitting light. Light shining into one end of the fiber travels through the glass to the other end. The effect is similar to electrons that carry a signal in copper wire. When you speak into a telephone, the signal created by your voice is converted to light signals that travel through the glass fiber. At the other end, the light may be converted into electronic signals that can then be converted to sound.

A Bright Idea

Can you communicate using an optical fiber?

1. Construct a barrier between you and a partner so that you cannot see each other.
2. Run a plastic optical fiber past the barrier.
3. Bring the bulb of a penlight flashlight close to your end of the fiber.
4. Using a single flash for "yes" and two flashes for "no," send your partner a message by responding to a series of yes and no questions he or she asks.
5. Change roles so that your partner has a chance to send signals in response to your questions.

Observing What happened when you and your partner sent signals to each other?

Figure 16 Even if optical fibers are twisted into a loop, the light moves within the fibers.
Making Generalizations How can this property of optical fibers be useful?

You know that light can pass through glass from one side to the other. That's one reason you can see through a window. But when light moves through an optical fiber, it is reflected within the fiber. It doesn't pass through the outside surface. For this reason, there is little loss of light from one end to the other—an important condition for transmitting messages!

A pair of optical fibers, the thickness of a human hair, can carry 625,000 phone calls at one time. One quarter pound of glass fiber can replace over two tons of copper wire. This difference is a big advantage when installing long lines like those that carry messages under the ocean. Because optical fibers are so efficient, they are being used to replace most copper telephone and cable television lines. Another benefit of glass fiber is its stability. Since the glass does not corrode as metals do, the lines are easier to maintain.

Section 3 Review

1. What property of ceramics makes them useful as the walls for ovens or as insulating materials?
2. In what ways can the properties of glass be changed?
3. How is a message transmitted through a glass fiber?
4. **Thinking Critically Applying Concepts** Before ceramics were invented, people stored food in containers such as baskets, leather bags, and wooden bowls. What properties of ceramics made them better containers for food?

Check Your Progress

CHAPTER PROJECT 4

Devise a plan to test some chemical and physical properties of the polymers you have collected. Tests might include hardness, fiber strength, flexibility, color, density, solubility in water, or reaction to corrosive chemicals. Construct a data table on which you can record results of your tests.

SECTION 4 Radioactive Elements

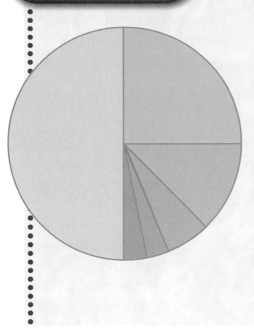

DISCOVER ·····························ACTIVITY···

How Much Goes Away?

1. Make a circle about 8–10 centimeters in diameter on a piece of paper. You can do this by tracing the rim of a round container.

2. Use a straightedge to draw a line dividing the circle in half. Then divide one half into quarters, then into eighths, and so on, as shown in the diagram.

3. ✂ With scissors, cut out your circle. Now cut away the undivided half circle. Next, cut away the undivided quarter circle. Continue until you are left with one segment.

4. Place the segments on your desktop in the order you cut them.

Think It Over

Making Models How is the piece of paper changing each time? Suppose the original circle was a model for a sample of radioactive material, and the paper you cut away is material that became nonradioactive. What would eventually happen?

More than a thousand years ago, some people came up with what they thought was a great idea. Take some dull, cheap lead metal and turn it into valuable gold! They heated the lead, cooled it, added acid to it. They ground it into a powder and mixed it with everything they could think of. Of course, nothing worked. There is no chemical reaction that converts one element into another.

Even so, elements do sometimes change into other elements. A uranium atom can become a thorium atom. Atoms of carbon can become atoms of nitrogen. (But lead never changes into gold, unfortunately!) How is it possible for these changes to happen?

GUIDE FOR READING

◆ What happens during radioactive decay?

◆ How is half-life a useful property of radioactive isotopes?

◆ In what ways are radioactive isotopes useful?

Reading Tip As you read, use the headings to make an outline about the properties and uses of radioactive isotopes.

Figure 17 This painting from 1570 shows people trying to change lead into gold. No such chemical reaction was ever accomplished.

Chapter 4 **L ◆ 133**

Carbon-12

Mass number ↗12
Atomic number ↘6 C

Carbon-14

Mass number ↗14
Atomic number ↘6 C

Figure 18 All carbon atoms have 6 protons in each nucleus, but the isotope carbon-12 has 6 neutrons and the isotope carbon-14 has 8 neutrons.

Figure 19 Radioactive elements give off mass and energy during radioactive decay. *Interpreting Diagrams Which type of decay does not result in a different element?*

Nuclear Reactions

You have already learned that an atom consists of a nucleus of protons and neutrons, surrounded by a cloud of electrons. A chemical change always involves the electrons but doesn't affect the nucleus. Since the number of protons determines the identity of the atom, one element can't be made into another element by a chemical reaction. Such a change happens only during **nuclear reactions** (NOO klee ur)—reactions involving the particles in the nucleus of an atom.

Isotopes

Remember that all the atoms of an element have the same number of protons (same atomic number), but the number of neutrons can vary. Atoms with the same number of protons and different numbers of neutrons are called **isotopes** (EYE suh tohps).

To show the difference between isotopes of the same element, you write both the name of the element and the mass number of the isotope. **Mass number** is the sum of the protons and neutrons in the nucleus of an atom. Consider, for example, isotopes of carbon. Most carbon atoms are carbon-12, having six protons and six neutrons (and six electrons). About one out of every trillion carbon atoms, however, has eight neutrons. That isotope is carbon-14. Figure 18 shows you how to write the symbol for the two isotopes. Note that the atomic number is included, too.

☑ *Checkpoint Why do mass numbers for isotopes differ?*

Radioactive Decay

Some isotopes are unstable. The nucleus of an unstable atom does not hold together well. Unstable isotopes undergo nuclear reactions, often forming atoms with different atomic numbers or atomic masses. In a process called **radioactive decay,** the atomic nuclei of unstable isotopes release fast-moving particles and energy. There are three types of radioactive decay, each determined by the type of radiation released by the unstable

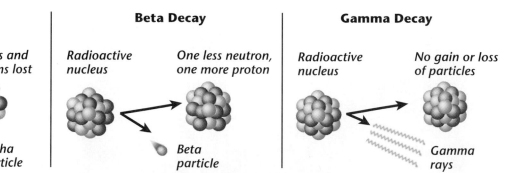

Alpha Decay

Radioactive nucleus → 2 protons and 2 neutrons lost

Alpha particle

Beta Decay

Radioactive nucleus → One less neutron, one more proton

Beta particle

Gamma Decay

Radioactive nucleus → No gain or loss of particles

Gamma rays

nucleus. **Radioactive decay can produce alpha particles, beta particles, and gamma rays.** (Alpha, beta, and gamma are the first three letters of the Greek alphabet.) The particles and energy produced during radioactive decay are forms of **nuclear radiation.**

Alpha Decay An **alpha particle** consists of two protons and two neutrons. It is the same as a helium nucleus. Release of an alpha particle by an atom decreases the atomic number by 2 and the mass number by 4. Although alpha particles move very fast, they are stopped by collisions with atoms. Alpha radiation can cause an injury much like a bad burn. But a sheet of paper or thin piece of metal foil will act as a shield.

Beta Decay When a neutron inside the nucleus of an unstable atom breaks apart, it forms a beta particle and a proton. A **beta particle** is an electron given off by a nucleus during radioactive decay. The new proton remains inside the nucleus. That means that the nucleus now has one less neutron and one more proton. Its mass number remains the same, but its atomic number increases by 1.

Beta particles travel much faster than alpha particles. They can pass through an aluminum sheet 3 millimeters thick. They can also travel into the human body and damage its cells.

Gamma Decay Alpha and beta decay are almost always accompanied by gamma radiation. **Gamma radiation** is high-energy waves, similar to X-rays. Gamma radiation (also called gamma rays) does not cause a change in either the atomic mass or the atomic number of the atom formed. But the energy released is the most penetrating type of radiation. You would need a piece of lead several centimeters thick or a concrete wall about a meter thick to stop gamma rays. They can pass right through a human body, causing severe damage to cells.

Sharpen your Skills

Predicting ACTIVITY

Look at the table of radioactive isotopes below.

Isotope	Type of Decay
$^{238}_{92}U$	Alpha
$^{63}_{28}Ni$	Beta
$^{131}_{53}I$	Beta
$^{226}_{88}Ra$	Alpha

1. With the help of a periodic table (see Appendix D), predict the element that forms in each case.
2. Label the symbol for each new element. Include the atomic number and mass number.

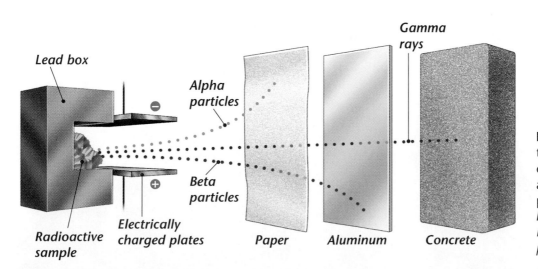

Figure 20 The three types of nuclear radiation can be separated according to charge and penetrating power. *Inferring Which type of radiation is the most penetrating?*

Half-Lives of Some Radioactive Elements	
Element	**Half-Life**
Carbon-14	5,730 years
Chlorine-36	400,000 years
Cobalt-60	5.26 years
Iodine-131	8.07 days
Phosphorus-32	14.3 days
Polonium-216	0.16 second
Radium-226	1,600 years
Sodium-24	15 hours
Uranium-235	710 million years
Uranium-238	4.5 billion years

Figure 21 The half-lives of radioactive elements vary greatly. *Interpreting Data* Which isotope in this table decays most rapidly?

Half-Life

Not all the atoms of a sample of a radioactive isotope decay at once. They decay randomly, one at a time. If you watched a sample of iodine-131, for example, you couldn't predict when any particular nucleus would decay. But the time it takes for half the atoms to change can be measured. The **half-life** of an isotope is the length of time needed for half the mass of a sample to decay. Half-life is different for each isotope. As you can see from Figure 21, half-lives can range from less than a second to billions of years!

INTEGRATING EARTH SCIENCE Fossils are the traces or remains of living things that have been preserved. **The half-lives of certain radioactive isotopes are useful in determining the ages of rocks and fossils.** For example, as plants grow they use carbon dioxide (CO_2) from the air. Some carbon dioxide contains carbon-14. This becomes part of the plant's structures the same way carbon-12 does. After the plant dies, it stops taking in carbon dioxide. If the plant's remains are preserved as a fossil, the amount of carbon-14 present can be measured. From the data, scientists can calculate how many half-lives have passed since the plant was alive. This process is called **radioactive dating.**

The half-life of carbon-14 is short compared to some other radioactive isotopes. It cannot be used to find the ages of objects older than about 60,000 years. Other isotopes, such as potassium-40 and uranium-238, are used to study older fossils, rocks, and objects used by early humans.

☑ *Checkpoint* How does the mass of a radioactive sample change after one half-life?

Figure 22 Using the known half-lives of certain radioactive elements, such as carbon-14 and uranium-238, scientists can determine the age of ancient objects. This saber-toothed cat lived about 25 million years ago.

Phosphorus-32

Phosphorus-32
in leaves

Figure 23 Phosphorus-32 added to soil is absorbed through the plant's roots. The tracer can be detected in any plant structures in which the phosphorus is used.

Using Radioactive Isotopes

In addition to studying objects from the past, people use radioactive isotopes for work in the present. **Radioactive isotopes are useful both as sources of radiation and as tracers.** The radiation released by radioactive isotopes is itself useful. Nuclear power plants and some medical treatments, for example, depend on nuclear reactions as sources of radiation.

Another important use depends on the fact that the radiation given off by isotopes can be detected. Like a lighthouse flashing in the night, a radioactive isotope "signals" where it is. **Tracers** are radioactive isotopes that can be followed through the steps of a chemical reaction or industrial process. In chemical reactions, tracers behave the same way as nonradioactive forms of an element.

Tracers in Chemical Reactions Scientists can make use of tracers in chemical reactions. Equipment that detects radiation can track the tracer wherever it goes. This technique is helpful for studying reactions in living organisms. For example, phosphorus is used by plants in small amounts for healthy growth. A plant will absorb radioactive phosphorus-32 added to the soil just as it does the nonradioactive form. Radiation will be present in any part of the plant that contains the isotope. In this way, biologists can learn where and how plants use phosphorus.

Uses in Industry Radioactive isotopes are valuable in industry as tracers and for the radiation they produce. For example, tracers are used in finding weak spots in metal pipes, especially oil pipelines. When added to a liquid, tracers can easily be detected if they leak out of the lines.

Engineers use gamma radiation from radioactive isotopes to look for flaws in metal. Gamma rays can pass through metal and be detected on a photographic film. This is similar to using X-rays to take a picture inside your body. By looking at the

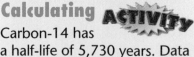

Calculating **ACTIVITY**
Carbon-14 has a half-life of 5,730 years. Data from several newly discovered fossils shows that carbon-14 has undergone decay in the fossils for five half-lives. Calculate the age of the fossils.

Figure 24 The radioactive isotope technetium-99 is used in medical studies of the heart, lungs, liver, and bones. **A.** In these healthy lungs, the red areas show greater absorption of the isotope than the yellow or green areas. **B.** In the hand, the bones are colored orange.

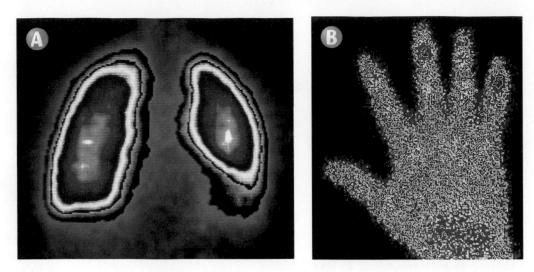

Social Studies
CONNECTION

Using radioactive materials can provide benefits such as electricity or advanced medical care. But what happens to the unavoidable radioactive waste? People aren't so comfortable having that around!

NIMBY is short for the phrase "not in my backyard." It stands for the idea that people don't want unpleasant or possible hazardous conditions near where they live. They would prefer to see radioactive wastes go elsewhere.

In Your Journal

Your local government has invited citizens to a meeting to discuss possible options for storing radioactive wastes from nearby medical or industrial uses. Write a one- or two-paragraph speech to the public meeting, expressing your opinion.

gamma-ray images, structural engineers can detect small cracks in the metal of bridges and building frames. Without these images, a problem might not be discovered until a disaster occurs.

Uses in Medicine Doctors use radioactive isotopes to detect *INTEGRATING HEALTH* medical problems and to treat some diseases. Tracers injected into the body travel to organs and other structures where that chemical is normally used. Using equipment that detects radiation, technicians make images of the bone, blood vessel, or organ affected. For example, tracers made with technetium-99 are frequently used to diagnose problems in the bones, liver, kidneys, and digestive system. Other isotopes, such as thallium-201 in the heart and xenon-133 in the lungs, help doctors diagnose disease in these organs.

In a process called **radiation therapy,** radioactive elements are used to destroy unhealthy cells. Iodine-131, for example, is given to patients with tumors of the thyroid gland, a gland in the neck that controls the rate at which nutrients are used. Because the thyroid gland uses iodine, the radioactive iodine-131 collects in the gland. Radiation from this isotope destroys unwanted cells in the gland without serious effects on other parts of the body.

Cancer tumors of different kinds often are treated from outside the body with high-energy gamma rays. Many hospitals use cobalt-60 for this purpose. When gamma radiation is focused on a cancer tumor, it causes changes that kill the cancer cells.

Nuclear Power Nuclear reactions release enormous quantities of energy compared to chemical reactions. For this reason, some power plants use radioactive isotopes as fuel. Carefully controlled reactions, most often using uranium-235, provide electric power in many parts of the world.

✓ *Checkpoint* What is a tracer?

Figure 25 Waste Isolation Pilot Plant (WIPP) is a site in New Mexico where the United States government is developing safe storage for radioactive wastes. Large underground rooms (left), will house the wastes in secure barrels (right).

Safe Use of Radioactive Materials

Despite the positive uses for radioactive materials, they also are dangerous. Radiation penetrates living tissue, knocking electrons from atoms. This process produces ions that then can interfere with chemical reactions in living cells. Illness, disease, and even death may result from overexposure to radiation.

The dangers of radioactive materials mean that their use must be carefully managed. People who work with these materials must wear protective clothing and use insulating shields. Radioactive wastes can't just be thrown away. After radiation therapy, for example, contaminated equipment and clothing can still be hazardous. These items must be disposed of properly. Materials with low levels of radiation may be buried in landfills. Such landfills are carefully monitored to prevent contamination of the environment. Isotopes with long half-lives, however, will remain hazardous for hundreds or even thousand of years. Plans are under way to dispose of these kinds of materials in specially designed containers that will be buried in very dry underground tunnels. In that way the radioactive wastes can be isolated for many generations.

Section 4 Review

1. Describe the three types of radiation given off during radioactive decay.
2. How are radioactive isotopes helpful for studying rocks and fossils?
3. Give two examples of how tracers are used. Tell why radioactive isotopes work as tracers.
4. **Thinking Critically Making Judgments** If there were a proposal in your state to ban the use of radioactive materials because of the hazards of radioactive waste, would you support the idea? Why or why not?

Check Your Progress

CHAPTER PROJECT 4

After your teacher approves your plan, perform your tests. Record all results in your data table. If there is time, perform your tests more than once to obtain multiple sets of data. Try to organize your samples into groups based on the results of your tests. Identify similarities and differences among the groups.

Making Models

THAT'S HALF-LIFE!

In this lab, you will use pennies to model how half-life is related to the decay of radioactive isotopes.

Problem

How does a sample of radioactive waste decay to a nonhazardous level?

Materials

100 pennies
container such as a jar or a box
colored pencils (optional)
graph paper

Procedure

1. Place 100 pennies in a container. Mix them up and then shake them out onto the desktop.
2. Separate the pennies showing heads from those showing tails.
3. Count the number of pennies showing tails and calculate the number of pennies showing heads. Record both these values.
4. Put back only the pennies showing tails.
5. Repeat Steps 2–4 until there are two or fewer pennies left in the container.
6. Keep a tally of the total number of pennies removed from the container. Record this number after each trial.

Analyze and Conclude

1. Make a graph of your data. Label the horizontal axis with the trial number. Label the vertical axis with the number of pennies left in the container after each trial. Connect the data points with a smooth, curved line.
2. What does the graph tell you?
3. On the same set of axes, plot the total number of pennies removed from the container after each trial. Use a dotted line or different colored pencil to make this graph.
4. What does your second graph tell you?
5. Suppose the pennies represent nuclei of a radioactive element. What do you think the heads and tails represent?
6. What do you think is represented by each trial or shake of the pennies?
7. How many half-lives does it take for the substance modeled in this lab to decay to two or fewer "nuclei"?
8. **Think About It** Suppose 1,600 grams of low-level radioactive waste is buried at a waste disposal site. Assuming that 10 grams of radioactive material is an acceptable level of radiation exposure, about how many half-lives must pass before there is no longer a health risk at the site?

More to Explore

How could you use this model to show the decay of a sample that was twice as massive as the sample used in this lab? What would you do differently? Predict how you think the results would differ.

DATA TABLE

Trial	Tails Remaining	Heads Removed (each trial)	Total Pennies Removed
1			
2			
3			

SECTION 1 — Polymers and Composites

Key Ideas
◆ Carbon atoms form chemical bonds with as many as four other atoms. Carbon atoms can link to each other, forming long chains, branches, and rings.
◆ Polymers are large carbon compounds. A polymer is made of many small molecules called monomers.
◆ Polymers occur naturally as products of living cells. Polymers also are synthesized in factories and laboratories for a variety of uses.
◆ Composite materials combine the useful properties of two different substances.

Key Terms
polymer
monomer
cellulose
plastic
composite

SECTION 2 — Metals and Alloys
INTEGRATING TECHNOLOGY

Key Ideas
◆ An alloy is a mixture of two or more elements, one of which is a metal. Alloys have the properties of metals, but also have other properties that make them more useful than the metals alone.
◆ Steel is one of the most frequently used alloys. Its strength and resistance to corrosion make it suitable for use in such things as building materials, tools, and machinery.

Key Term
alloy

SECTION 3 — Ceramics and Glass

Key Ideas
◆ Ceramics are made by heating clay mixed with other materials to temperatures that produce a brittle, crystalline solid. Food storage, building materials, and heat insulators are some uses of ceramics.
◆ Glass results when sand is melted to make a thick liquid that can be shaped when hot. Adding other materials gives glass properties such as heat resistance and color.
◆ Optical fibers are threadlike pieces of glass that transmit information in the form of light signals.

Key Terms
ceramics   glass   optical fiber

SECTION 4 — Radioactive Elements

Key Ideas
◆ Radioactive decay is a change in the nucleus of an atom that releases particles and energy. The products of radioactive decay are alpha and beta particles and gamma rays.
◆ Half-life is the amount of time it takes for half of the radioactive atoms of an isotope to decay.
◆ Radioactive isotopes are used as sources of radiation in industry, medicine, and research.

Key Terms
nuclear reaction   beta particle
isotope   gamma radiation
mass number   half-life
radioactive decay   radioactive dating
nuclear radiation   tracer
alpha particle   radiation therapy

USING THE INTERNET ACTIVITY
www.science-explorer.phschool.com

Reviewing Content

For more review of key concepts, see the Interactive Student Tutorial CD-ROM.

Multiple Choice

Choose the letter of the best answer.

1. A large molecule made of many monomers is called a
   a. plastic.
   b. polymer.
   c. protein.
   d. chain.

2. Fiberglass is a type of
   a. polymer.
   b. alloy.
   c. ceramic.
   d. composite.

3. The properties of alloys most resemble
   a. ceramics.
   b. glass.
   c. metals.
   d. polymers.

4. Clean sand is heated to its melting point to make
   a. ceramics.
   b. glass.
   c. alloys.
   d. composites.

5. Atoms that have the same atomic number but different mass numbers are
   a. radioactive.
   b. alloys.
   c. isotopes.
   d. alpha particles.

True or False

If the statement is true, write true. If it is false, change the underlined word or words to make the statement true.

6. <u>Oxygen</u> is the element that forms the backbone of most polymers.

7. Cellulose molecules are examples of <u>synthetic</u> polymers.

8. A useful alloy of copper and tin is <u>steel</u>.

9. The furnaces used to melt metals are insulated with <u>ceramic</u> materials.

10. Alpha, beta, and gamma radiation form as the result of <u>chemical reactions</u>.

Checking Concepts

11. Name some polymers that are products of nature. Tell where they come from.

12. Explain why some advantages of using polymers can become disadvantages.

13. List three properties of metals. Then for each property, give an example of how a specific metal is put to use.

14. Why is gold always mixed with other metals to make jewelry?

15. What is the purpose of the glaze on the surface of a pottery vase?

16. Explain why a chemical reaction cannot change one element into another element.

17. What properties of radioactive isotopes make them useful?

18. **Writing to Learn** You are a chemist. You invent a polymer that can be a substitute for a natural material such as wood, cotton, or leather. Write a short speech to make at a science conference, explaining why you think your polymer is a good replacement for the natural material.

Thinking Visually

19. **Compare/Contrast Table** Copy the table about polymers, alloys, ceramics, and glass onto a separate sheet of paper. Then complete it and add a title. (For more on compare/contrast tables see the Skills Handbook.)

Material	Made From	How Made	How Used
Polymers	Monomers (carbon compounds)	a. ?	b. ?
Alloys	c. ?	Metals heated and mixed	d. ?
Ceramics	Clay; other minerals	e. ?	f. ?
Glass	g. ?	Melted, then cooled in desired shapes	h. ?

Applying Skills

The diagram below shows the first few steps of the radioactive decay of uranium-238. Use the diagram to answer Questions 20–22.

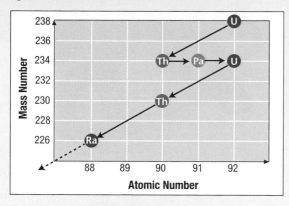

20. **Interpreting Data** How many elements are in the diagram? How many different isotopes of each element are there?
21. **Classifying** What type of radioactive decay resulted in uranium-238 becoming thorium-234? How do you know?
22. **Inferring** How do you know from the diagram that thorium-230 is radioactive?

Thinking Critically

23. **Applying Concepts** The earliest building bricks were dried by being left out in the sun. Why can this kind of brick be used only in areas with a dry climate?
24. **Comparing and Contrasting** Explain which material—steel, glass or polystyrene foam—would be the best choice for each of the following uses: cup for hot chocolate; hammer; wall of a salt-water aquarium; egg carton.
25. **Making Judgments** The plastic rings that hold beverage cans together are sometimes hazardous to living things in the ocean. Do you think companies that make soft drinks should be allowed to continue using plastic rings? Consider what could replace them and the effects of the change.
26. **Calculating** A wooden tool found in a cave has one fourth as much carbon-14 as a living tree. How old is the tool? (*Hint:* The half-life of carbon-14 is 5,730 years.)

Performance Assessment

CHAPTER PROJECT 4 — Wrap Up

Present Your Project Prepare a chart or poster to display the polymers you examined. Provide a sample of each polymer and include information such as its name, where it was found, what monomers it is made of (if known), and significant physical and chemical properties as shown by your tests. Be prepared to compare the polymers with other types of materials such as glass, ceramics, and metals.

Reflect and Record In your journal, explain how you might improve your collection and testing process. Describe one of the more interesting polymers that you found. Why do you think it is interesting?

Getting Involved

In Your Home Look for items in your home that can be made from more than one kind of material. (For example, a toothbrush holder may be made of plastic, metal, or ceramics.) Make a list of the items and what they are made of. Find out if these items can be made from still other materials. Develop a table that compares the advantages and disadvantages of using different materials for the same purpose.

BREAD ON THE RISE

HAVE YOU EVER . . .
- ♦ WATCHED BREAD RISING IN A PAN?
- ♦ TASTED A FRESHLY BAKED SLICE?
- ♦ NOTICED DIFFERENT-SIZED HOLES IN BREAD?
- ♦ WONDERED WHY THE HOLES ARE THERE?

A San Ildefonso Pueblo woman and child test their bread made in an outside oven.

Bread is one of the first foods known. It's eaten all over the world. Because it is a main source of nutrition for many people, bread is sometimes called the "staff of life." Flour, water, and salt are the basic ingredients of most breads. Usually bread also contains a leavening agent— an ingredient that makes the bread "rise."

To vary the taste, this simple bread mix is often changed in a variety of ways. Different kinds of flour and liquids as well as other ingredients, such as eggs, fruits, nuts, and spices, all change the flavor.

There are three types of bread. Flat breads, such as pita, don't have any leavening agent— thus the name "flat." Quick breads, such as biscuits, rise because they're made with the chemicals baking soda or baking powder. Yeast breads, such as whole wheat and rye bread, are make with a living organism—yeast—which causes the bread to rise. How many of these breads do you eat?

Flat Breads Around the World

Have you ever eaten pita bread? A tortilla? Matzo? These breads share a history that is older than any other kind of bread. They are all flat breads that originated among specific peoples in different parts of the world.

People made flat bread long before the leavening properties of yeast were discovered and even longer before chemical leavening agents were found. Nearly 12,000 years ago, people learned how to crush grains, add water, and bake dough on hot stones. In the ruins of an ancient village in Switzerland, scientists found a piece of flat bread more than 4,000 years old.

The ingredients in flat breads—and other breads as well—usually depend on the kinds of grains people grow. Grains such as wheat, corn, barley, buckwheat, and millet are all common ingredients. Today, flat breads made of these grains are the basic foods in many people's diets. Here are some traditional flat breads.

Matzo is a flat bread made from flour, which Jews eat most often during the religious holiday of Passover.

- People in Greece and Middle Eastern countries, such as Syria, Lebanon, and Jordan, eat pita bread, a round bread with a large pocket inside.

- Scandinavians sometimes eat a traditional flat bread called lefse. It can be made with flour or potatoes.

- In Mexico and Central America, the traditional flat bread is the tortilla, made of cornmeal.

- During the holiday of Passover, Jews around the world eat matzo, a cracker-like flat bread.

- People in Brazil eat flat cakes made from the root of the cassava plant.

- Millet cakes and a flat bread called chapati are widely eaten in India.

Papadum, an Indian flat bread

Social Studies Activity

On a world map, locate some of the countries and regions where flat breads are eaten: Middle Eastern countries, Greece, Mexico, Central America, Brazil, India, and South Africa. With a partner, learn more about one of the flat breads mentioned here. Or choose another kind of bread. Find out how the bread is made and eaten.

- What are the primary ingredients of the bread? What grain is used?
- What do people eat on or with the bread?
- Is the bread usually eaten every day, during a certain season, or on holidays?
- In what countries are the breads most frequently eaten?

Science

Quick Breads

Most of the bread you eat needs to rise before it is baked. Why is rising necessary? How does it happen?

Flour and water mixed together are the basis of bread. But this dough is dense. A leavening agent is needed to make the dough rise so it's less dense. The leavening agent works by producing carbon dioxide gas (CO_2), which then expands as it is heated. Hundreds of tiny bubbles enlarge and lift the dough. The spaces made by the bubbles are baked into the bread.

Most quick breads use either baking soda or baking powder as leavening agents. Baking soda and baking powder are very similar. Which one you use depends on the other ingredients in the recipe.

Baking soda is a chemical compound, also called sodium bicarbonate ($NaHCO_3$). As baking soda is heated, it decomposes into carbon dioxide gas and sodium hydroxide:

$$NaHCO_3 \rightarrow CO_2 + NaOH$$

Bran, blueberry, and raisin muffins are forms of quick breads.

Sodium hydroxide is a base. It can give an unpleasant, soapy taste to the bread. Therefore, the recipe needs to include an acidic ingredient. Orange juice, lemon juice, sour cream, and buttermilk contain weak acids. The acid in any one of these ingredients neutralizes the sodium hydroxide. Some breads taste better with acidic ingredients. However, there are many quick breads that are made without acids. These breads often use baking powder.

Baking powder has baking soda as its main ingredient. It also includes one or more acidic compounds, such as cream of tartar. The cream of tartar neutralizes the base that forms. Another ingredient in baking powder—cornstarch—keeps the compounds from clumping. Baking powder can be used in recipes that don't have an acidic ingredient.

Science Activity

Set up an experiment to measure the amount of carbon dioxide released by 3 leavening agents—yeast, baking soda, and baking powder.

◆ Fill 4 test tubes with equal amounts of warm water, between 38°C and 46°C. The water in each test tube should be the same temperature. Add $\frac{1}{2}$ teaspoon of granulated sugar to each test tube. Shake to dissolve.

◆ Add a teaspoon of one leavening agent per test tube (except for the control): active dry yeast, baking soda, and baking powder.

◆ Quickly attach a large balloon to each test tube. All balloons should be the same size. Gently shake each test tube to mix solid and water.

◆ Measure the circumference of each balloon after 5 minutes and then again after 15 minutes. Record your results.

Which ingredient caused the balloon to expand the fastest? Which ingredient caused a slow change in the balloon size? Therefore, which ingredient gave off the most CO_2?

How Yeast Works

Yeast is different from other leavening agents because it is actually a one-celled living organism whose activities produce carbon dioxide. Yeast breads include white and whole wheat breads as well as French and Italian bread. Rye bread and black breads are yeast breads that originated in Germany, Russia, and Scandinavia.

In yeast bread recipes, water and flour are mixed by stirring or kneading. As a result, proteins in the flour interconnect. The mixture develops long, strong, elastic strands of a new substance called gluten. Flour contains an enzyme, which breaks starch molecules in the flour into simple sugars. The yeast cells feed on simple sugars in the flour and begin to reproduce. One of the products of this process is carbon dioxide. The carbon dioxide gas forms air bubbles in the dough, causing it to expand. The gluten stretches but does not allow the bubbles to escape. So, the bread rises.

Bread dough is shaped into loaves before it is baked.

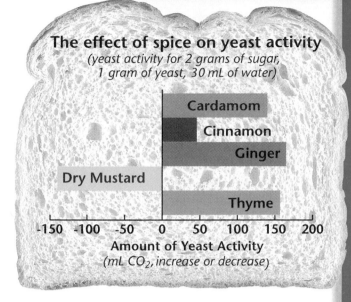

The effect of spice on yeast activity
(yeast activity for 2 grams of sugar, 1 gram of yeast, 30 mL of water)

Cardamom
Cinnamon
Ginger
Dry Mustard
Thyme

-150 -100 -50 0 50 100 150 200

Amount of Yeast Activity
(mL CO_2, increase or decrease)

For flavor, other ingredients, including spices, are often added. But spices in yeast breads can do more than just add flavor. Certain amounts of some spices can actually help yeast grow and release more carbon dioxide gas. Some spices— such as dry mustard—reduce yeast growth. The bar graph on this page shows how yeast activity will increase or decrease when different spices are added to a mixture of 2 grams sugar, 1 gram yeast, and 30 milliliters water.

Math Activity

Read the bar graph to answer the questions below. The effects of five spices are shown: cardamom, cinnamon, ginger, dry mustard, and thyme. For each spice, the amount added is 0.5 gram. The vertical line in the middle of the graph shows the amount of yeast activity before any spices are added.

◆ Which spice increased yeast activity the most?

◆ Which spice decreased yeast activity?

◆ About how much greater was the change in yeast activity for ginger than for cardamom?

◆ How much did yeast activity increase when thyme was added? About how much greater was the change in activity for thyme compared to cinnamon?

◆ What do you think would happen if 1 gram of cinnamon were added instead of 0.5 gram?

A Family Tradition

In some families, traditions are handed down from one generation to another for years. Even the way something is made can be passed on, such as when an older person shows a younger one the secrets of a special recipe.

In this article, Janet Knickerbocker describes how her grandmother passed on the family bread recipe to the author. (*Note:* A bread sack may have been made from a cloth flour sack.)

GRANDMA MADE THE BREAD

Grandma always made the bread.

For every occasion, we could always count on those crusty loaves, sliced and slathered thick with butter.

Grandma always made the bread.

Now, Grandma had some peculiar ways. She was always saving this or that, slightly used pieces of tinfoil, bits of string, and bread sacks. Bread sacks. How I hated those. Carrying lunch to school in a bread sack. All the other children had shiny lunch pails where nothing got squashed together. But every time Grandma came for a visit, she packed our lunches and off we went, bread sack in hand.

Grandma always made the bread.

Grandma decided another family member should learn to make "the bread." As she gathered the ingredients and placed them in the bowl she explained each step.

"Heat the milk, just so. Add the butter and eggs now." Then came the flour, scoop after scoop. She deftly worked it into a smooth ball. Then she scraped the bowl with her hand, to gather each tiny bit of the dough. "We will need this," she said.

Suddenly, I realized why Grandma was a saver of oddities, why she went around snapping lights off and scolding us gently for being wasteful. Grandma had never had "enough" of anything in her life. Those tiny scraps of dough could help feed another hungry mouth, for whom bread had not been a treat, but a necessity. I felt very small.

Language Arts Activity

Think about a tradition passed down in your family. It might be something that began long ago, with your grandparents or even earlier. Or it might be a newer tradition, such as one started by your parents. Write a description of this tradition. Express what it means to you by using concrete sensory details in your description.

The years have passed. Everything has changed, except Grandma. She always makes the bread, still saves bits of this and that in her starched apron pocket. I grew up and now I have a son.

The other day, I was making the bread. I instructed my small child how to heat the milk, just so. "Add the butter and eggs now." Then we added scoop after scoop of flour. We worked until we had a smooth ball of dough. Then we scraped the bowl with our hands, to gather each tiny bit. "We will need this," I stated matter-of-factly.

The smell of baking bread filled our little house as the bread sacks dried on the clothesline.

—*from "Grandma Made the Bread," in* Countryside and Small Stock Journal, *by Janet Knickerbocker*

Tie It Together

Make Your Own Bread

One of the best ways to learn about bread is to make it yourself. Work as a class to make the Irish whole-wheat soda bread recipe on this page. Or work in groups to find other bread recipes to make.

- ◆ Take turns kneading the dough.
- ◆ Try to determine when leavening agents are working in your bread.
- ◆ After the bread has cooled, examine a slice of it closely. How big are the bubbles of carbon dioxide gas in your slice of bread?

Irish Soda Bread

3 cups whole-wheat flour

1 cup all-purpose flour

1 tablespoon salt

1 teaspoon baking soda

$\frac{3}{4}$ teaspoon double-acting baking powder

$1\frac{2}{3}$ cups buttermilk

Combine the dry ingredients and mix thoroughly.
Add buttermilk to make a soft dough.
Knead on a lightly floured board for 2 or 3 minutes.
Form into a round loaf and place in a well-buttered 8-inch cake pan.
Bake in a preheated oven at 375°F for 35 to 40 minutes.
Let the loaf cool before cutting very thin slices.

Think Like a Scientist

Although you may not know it, you think like a scientist every day. Whenever you ask a question and explore possible answers, you use many of the same skills that scientists do. Some of these skills are described on this page.

Observing

When you use one or more of your five senses to gather information about the world, you are **observing.** Hearing a dog bark, counting twelve green seeds, and smelling smoke are all observations. To increase the power of their senses, scientists sometimes use microscopes, telescopes, or other instruments that help them make more detailed observations.

An observation must be factual and accurate—an exact report of what your senses detect. It is important to keep careful records of your observations in science class by writing or drawing in a notebook. The information collected through observations is called evidence, or data.

Inferring

When you explain or interpret an observation, you are **inferring,** or making an inference. For example, if you hear your dog barking, you may infer that someone is at your front door. To make this inference, you combine the evidence—the barking dog—and your experience or knowledge—you know that your dog barks when strangers approach—to reach a logical conclusion.

Notice that an inference is not a fact; it is only one of many possible explanations for an observation. For example, your dog may be barking because it wants to go for a walk. An inference may turn out to be incorrect even if it is based on accurate observations and logical reasoning. The only way to find out if an inference is correct is to investigate further.

Predicting

When you listen to the weather forecast, you hear many predictions about the next day's weather—what the temperature will be, whether it will rain, and how windy it will be. Weather forecasters use observations and knowledge of weather patterns to predict the weather. The skill of **predicting** involves making an inference about a future event based on current evidence or past experience.

Because a prediction is an inference, it may prove to be false. In science class, you can test some of your predictions by doing experiments. For example, suppose you predict that larger paper airplanes can fly farther than smaller airplanes. How could you test your prediction?

ACTIVITY Use the photograph to answer the questions below.

Observing Look closely at the photograph. List at least three observations.

Inferring Use your observations to make an inference about what has happened. What experience or knowledge did you use to make the inference?

Predicting Predict what will happen next. On what evidence or experience do you base your prediction?

Classifying

Could you imagine searching for a book in the library if the books were shelved in no particular order? Your trip to the library would be an all-day event! Luckily, librarians group together books on similar topics or by the same author. Grouping together items that are alike in some way is called **classifying.** You can classify items in many ways: by size, by shape, by use, and by other important characteristics.

Like librarians, scientists use the skill of classifying to organize information and objects. When things are sorted into groups, the relationships among them become easier to understand.

ACTIVITY
Classify the objects in the photograph into two groups based on any characteristic you choose. Then use another characteristic to classify the objects into three groups.

Making Models

Have you ever drawn a picture to help someone understand what you were saying? Such a drawing is one type of model. A model is a picture, diagram, computer image, or other representation of a complex object or process. **Making models** helps people understand things that they cannot observe directly.

Scientists often use models to represent things that are either very large or very small, such as the planets in the solar system, or the parts of a cell. Such models are physical models—drawings or three-dimensional structures that look like the real thing. Other models are mental models—mathematical equations or words that describe how something works.

ACTIVITY
This student is using a model to demonstrate what causes day and night on Earth. What do the flashlight and the tennis ball in the model represent?

Communicating

Whenever you talk on the phone, write a letter, or listen to your teacher at school, you are communicating. **Communicating** is the process of sharing ideas and information with other people. Communicating effectively requires many skills, including writing, reading, speaking, listening, and making models.

Scientists communicate to share results, information, and opinions. Scientists often communicate about their work in journals, over the telephone, in letters, and on the Internet. They also attend scientific meetings where they share their ideas with one another in person.

ACTIVITY
On a sheet of paper, write out clear, detailed directions for tying your shoe. Then exchange directions with a partner. Follow your partner's directions exactly. How successful were you at tying your shoe? How could your partner have communicated more clearly?

Making Measurements

When scientists make observations, it is not sufficient to say that something is "big" or "heavy." Instead, scientists use instruments to measure just how big or heavy an object is. By measuring, scientists can express their observations more precisely and communicate more information about what they observe.

Measuring in SI

The standard system of measurement used by scientists around the world is known as the International System of Units, which is abbreviated as SI (in French, *Système International d'Unités*). SI units are easy to use because they are based on multiples of 10. Each unit is ten times larger than the next smallest unit and one tenth the size of the next largest unit. The table lists the prefixes used to name the most common SI units.

Common SI Prefixes

Prefix	Symbol	Meaning
kilo-	k	1,000
hecto-	h	100
deka-	da	10
deci-	d	0.1 (one tenth)
centi-	c	0.01 (one hundredth)
milli-	m	0.001 (one thousandth)

Length To measure length, or the distance between two points, the unit of measure is the **meter (m).** One meter is the approximate distance from the floor to a doorknob. Long distances, such as the distance between two cities, are measured in kilometers (km). Small lengths are measured in centimeters (cm) or millimeters (mm). Scientists use metric rulers and meter sticks to measure length.

Common Conversions

1 km = 1,000 m
1 m = 100 cm
1 m = 1,000 mm
1 cm = 10 mm

The larger lines on the metric ruler in the picture show centimeter divisions, while the smaller, unnumbered lines show millimeter divisions. How many centimeters long is the shell? How many millimeters long is it?

Liquid Volume To measure the volume of a liquid, or the amount of space it takes up, you will use a unit of measure known as the **liter (L).** One liter is the approximate volume of a medium-sized carton of milk. Smaller volumes are measured in milliliters (mL). Scientists use graduated cylinders to measure liquid volume.

Common Conversion

1 L = 1,000 mL

The graduated cylinder in the picture is marked in milliliter divisions. Notice that the water in the cylinder has a curved surface. This curved surface is called the *meniscus.* To measure the volume, you must read the level at the lowest point of the meniscus. What is the volume of water in this graduated cylinder?

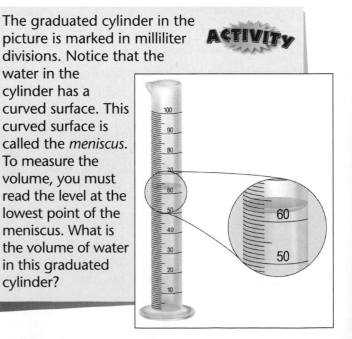

Mass To measure mass, or the amount of matter in an object, you will use a unit of measure known as the **gram (g)**. One gram is approximately the mass of a paper clip. Larger masses are measured in kilograms (kg). Scientists use a balance to find the mass of an object.

Common Conversion

1 kg = 1,000 g

The electronic balance displays the mass of an apple in kilograms. What is the mass of the apple? Suppose a recipe for applesauce called for one kilogram of apples. About how many apples would you need?

ACTIVITY

Temperature
To measure the temperature of a substance, you will use the **Celsius scale**. Temperature is measured in degrees Celsius (°C) using a Celsius thermometer. Water freezes at 0°C and boils at 100°C.

ACTIVITY

What is the temperature of the liquid in degrees Celsius?

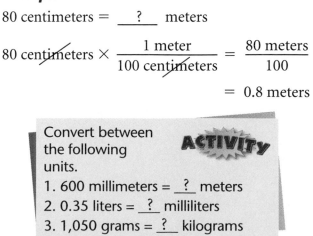

Converting SI Units

To use the SI system, you must know how to convert between units. Converting from one unit to another involves the skill of **calculating**, or using mathematical operations. Converting between SI units is similar to converting between dollars and dimes because both systems are based on multiples of ten.

Suppose you want to convert a length of 80 centimeters to meters. Follow these steps to convert between units.

1. Begin by writing down the measurement you want to convert—in this example, 80 centimeters.
2. Write a conversion factor that represents the relationship between the two units you are converting. In this example, the relationship is *1 meter = 100 centimeters*. Write this conversion factor as a fraction, making sure to place the units you are converting from (centimeters, in this example) in the denominator.

3. Multiply the measurement you want to convert by the fraction. When you do this, the units in the first measurement will cancel out with the units in the denominator. Your answer will be in the units you are converting to (meters, in this example).

Example

80 centimeters = ___?___ meters

$$80 \text{ centimeters} \times \frac{1 \text{ meter}}{100 \text{ centimeters}} = \frac{80 \text{ meters}}{100}$$
$$= 0.8 \text{ meters}$$

ACTIVITY

Convert between the following units.
1. 600 millimeters = _?_ meters
2. 0.35 liters = _?_ milliliters
3. 1,050 grams = _?_ kilograms

Conducting a Scientific Investigation

In some ways, scientists are like detectives, piecing together clues to learn about a process or event. One way that scientists gather clues is by carrying out experiments. An experiment tests an idea in a careful, orderly manner. Although all experiments do not follow the same steps in the same order, many follow a pattern similar to the one described here.

Posing Questions

Experiments begin by asking a scientific question. A scientific question is one that can be answered by gathering evidence. For example, the question "Which freezes faster—fresh water or salt water?" is a scientific question because you can carry out an investigation and gather information to answer the question.

Developing a Hypothesis

The next step is to form a hypothesis. A **hypothesis** is a prediction about the outcome of the experiment. Like all predictions, hypotheses are based on your observations and previous knowledge or experience. But, unlike many predictions, a hypothesis must be something that can be tested. A properly worded hypothesis should take the form of an *If . . . then . . .* statement. For example, a hypothesis might be *"If I add salt to fresh water, then the water will take longer to freeze."* A hypothesis worded this way serves as a rough outline of the experiment you should perform.

Designing an Experiment

Next you need to plan a way to test your hypothesis. Your plan should be written out as a step-by-step procedure and should describe the observations or measurements you will make.

Two important steps involved in designing an experiment are controlling variables and forming operational definitions.

Controlling Variables

In a well-designed experiment, you need to keep all variables the same except for one. A **variable** is any factor that can change in an experiment. The factor that you change is called the **manipulated variable.** In this experiment, the manipulated variable is the amount of salt added to the water. Other factors, such as the amount of water or the starting temperature, are kept constant.

The factor that changes as a result of the manipulated variable is called the responding variable. The **responding variable** is what you measure or observe to obtain your results. In this experiment, the responding variable is how long the water takes to freeze.

An experiment in which all factors except one are kept constant is a **controlled experiment.** Most controlled experiments include a test called the control. In this experiment, Container 3 is the control. Because no salt is added to Container 3, you can compare the results from the other containers to it. Any difference in results must be due to the addition of salt alone.

Forming Operational Definitions

Another important aspect of a well-designed experiment is having clear operational definitions. An **operational definition** is a statement that describes how a particular variable is to be measured or how a term is to be defined. For example, in this experiment, how will you determine if the water has frozen? You might decide to insert a stick in each container at the start of the experiment. Your operational definition of "frozen" would be the time at which the stick can no longer move.

EXPERIMENTAL PROCEDURE

1. Fill 3 containers with 300 milliliters of cold tap water.

2. Add 10 grams of salt to Container 1; stir. Add 20 grams of salt to Container 2; stir. Add no salt to Container 3.

3. Place the 3 containers in a freezer.

4. Check the containers every 15 minutes. Record your observations.

Interpreting Data

The observations and measurements you make in an experiment are called data. At the end of an experiment, you need to analyze the data to look for any patterns or trends. Patterns often become clear if you organize your data in a data table or graph. Then think through what the data reveal. Do they support your hypothesis? Do they point out a flaw in your experiment? Do you need to collect more data?

Drawing Conclusions

A conclusion is a statement that sums up what you have learned from an experiment. When you draw a conclusion, you need to decide whether the data you collected support your hypothesis or not. You may need to repeat an experiment several times before you can draw any conclusions from it. Conclusions often lead you to pose new questions and plan new experiments to answer them.

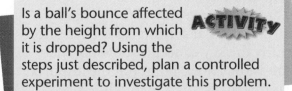

Is a ball's bounce affected by the height from which it is dropped? Using the steps just described, plan a controlled experiment to investigate this problem. **ACTIVITY**

Thinking Critically

Has a friend ever asked for your advice about a problem? If so, you may have helped your friend think through the problem in a logical way. Without knowing it, you used critical-thinking skills to help your friend. Critical thinking involves the use of reasoning and logic to solve problems or make decisions. Some critical-thinking skills are described below.

Comparing and Contrasting

When you examine two objects for similarities and differences, you are using the skill of **comparing and contrasting.** Comparing involves identifying similarities, or common characteristics. Contrasting involves identifying differences. Analyzing objects in this way can help you discover details that you might otherwise overlook.

Compare and contrast the two animals in the photo. First list all the similarities that you see. Then list all the differences. **ACTIVITY**

Applying Concepts

When you use your knowledge about one situation to make sense of a similar situation, you are using the skill of **applying concepts.** Being able to transfer your knowledge from one situation to another shows that you truly understand a concept. You may use this skill in answering test questions that present different problems from the ones you've reviewed in class.

You have just learned that water takes longer to freeze when other substances are mixed into it. Use this knowledge to explain why people need a substance called antifreeze in their car's radiator in the winter. **ACTIVITY**

Interpreting Illustrations

Diagrams, photographs, and maps are included in textbooks to help clarify what you read. These illustrations show processes, places, and ideas in a visual manner. The skill called **interpreting illustrations** can help you learn from these visual elements. To understand an illustration, take the time to study the illustration along with all the written information that accompanies it. Captions identify the key concepts shown in the illustration. Labels point out the important parts of a diagram or map, while keys identify the symbols used in a map.

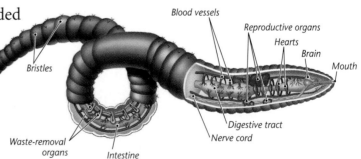

Blood vessels

Reproductive organs

Hearts

Brain

Mouth

Bristles

Digestive tract

Nerve cord

Waste-removal organs

Intestine

▲ **Internal anatomy of an earthworm**

Study the diagram above. Then write a short paragraph explaining what you have learned. **ACTIVITY**

Relating Cause and Effect

If one event causes another event to occur, the two events are said to have a cause-and-effect relationship. When you determine that such a relationship exists between two events, you use a skill called **relating cause and effect.** For example, if you notice an itchy, red bump on your skin, you might infer that a mosquito bit you. The mosquito bite is the cause, and the bump is the effect.

It is important to note that two events do not necessarily have a cause-and-effect relationship just because they occur together. Scientists carry out experiments or use past experience to determine whether a cause-and-effect relationship exists.

ACTIVITY

You are on a camping trip and your flashlight has stopped working. List some possible causes for the flashlight malfunction. How could you determine which cause-and-effect relationship has left you in the dark?

Making Generalizations

When you draw a conclusion about an entire group based on information about only some of the group's members, you are using a skill called **making generalizations.** For a generalization to be valid, the sample you choose must be large enough and representative of the entire group. You might, for example, put this skill to work at a farm stand if you see a sign that says, "Sample some grapes before you buy." If you sample a few sweet grapes, you may conclude that all the grapes are sweet—and purchase a large bunch.

ACTIVITY

A team of scientists needs to determine whether the water in a large reservoir is safe to drink. How could they use the skill of making generalizations to help them? What should they do?

Making Judgments

When you evaluate something to decide whether it is good or bad, or right or wrong, you are using a skill called **making judgments.** For example, you make judgments when you decide to eat healthful foods or to pick up litter in a park. Before you make a judgment, you need to think through the pros and cons of a situation, and identify the values or standards that you hold.

ACTIVITY

Should children and teens be required to wear helmets when bicycling? Explain why you feel the way you do.

Problem Solving

When you use critical-thinking skills to resolve an issue or decide on a course of action, you are using a skill called **problem solving.** Some problems, such as how to convert a fraction into a decimal, are straightforward. Other problems, such as figuring out why your computer has stopped working, are complex. Some complex problems can be solved using the trial and error method—try out one solution first, and if that doesn't work, try another. Other useful problem-solving strategies include making models and brainstorming possible solutions with a partner.

Organizing Information

As you read this textbook, how can you make sense of all the information it contains? Some useful tools to help you organize information are shown on this page. These tools are called *graphic organizers* because they give you a visual picture of a topic, showing at a glance how key concepts are related.

Concept Maps

Concept maps are useful tools for organizing information on broad topics. A concept map begins with a general concept and shows how it can be broken down into more specific concepts. In that way, relationships between concepts become easier to understand.

A concept map is constructed by placing concept words (usually nouns) in ovals and connecting them with linking words. Often, the most general concept word is placed at the top, and the words become more specific as you move downward. Often the linking words, which are written on a line extending between two ovals, describe the relationship between the two concepts they connect. If you follow any string of concepts and linking words down the map, it should read like a sentence.

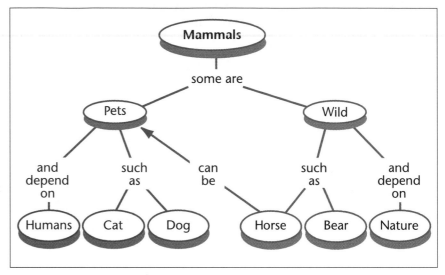

Some concept maps include linking words that connect a concept on one branch of the map to a concept on another branch. These linking words, called cross-linkages, show more complex interrelationships among concepts.

Compare/Contrast Tables

Compare/contrast tables are useful tools for sorting out the similarities and differences between two or more items. A table provides an organized framework in which to compare items based on specific characteristics that you identify.

To create a compare/contrast table, list the items to be compared across the top of a table. Then list the characteristics that will form the basis of your comparison in the left-hand column. Complete the table by filling in information about each characteristic, first for one item and then for the other.

Characteristic	Baseball	Basketball
Number of Players	9	5
Playing Field	Baseball diamond	Basketball court
Equipment	Bat, baseball, mitts	Basket, basketball

Venn Diagrams

Another way to show similarities and differences between items is with a Venn diagram. A Venn diagram consists of two or more circles that partially overlap. Each circle represents a particular concept or idea. Common characteristics, or similarities, are written within the area of overlap between the two circles. Unique characteristics, or differences, are written in the parts of the circles outside the area of overlap.

To create a Venn diagram, draw two overlapping circles. Label the circles with the names of the items being compared. Write the

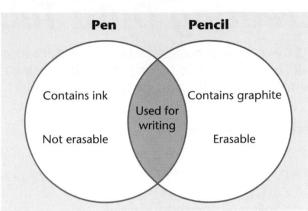

unique characteristics in each circle outside the area of overlap. Then write the shared characteristics within the area of overlap.

Flowcharts

A flowchart can help you understand the order in which certain events have occurred or should occur. Flowcharts are useful for outlining the stages in a process or the steps in a procedure.

To make a flowchart, write a brief description of each event in a box. Place the first event at the top of the page, followed by the second event, the third event, and so on. Then draw an arrow to connect each event to the one that occurs next.

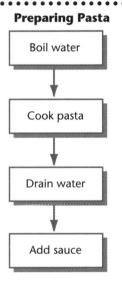

Cycle Diagrams

A cycle diagram can be used to show a sequence of events that is continuous, or cyclical. A continuous sequence does not have an end because, when the final event is over, the first event begins again. Like a flowchart, a cycle diagram can help you understand the order of events.

To create a cycle diagram, write a brief description of each event in a box. Place one event at the top of the page in the center. Then, moving in a clockwise direction around an imaginary circle, write each event in its proper sequence. Draw arrows that connect each event to the one that occurs next, forming a continuous circle.

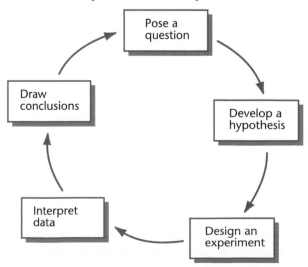

Creating Data Tables and Graphs

How can you make sense of the data in a science experiment? The first step is to organize the data to help you understand them. Data tables and graphs are helpful tools for organizing data.

Data Tables

You have gathered your materials and set up your experiment. But before you start, you need to plan a way to record what happens during the experiment. By creating a data table, you can record your observations and measurements in an orderly way.

Suppose, for example, that a scientist conducted an experiment to find out how many Calories people of different body masses burn while doing various activities. The data table shows the results.

Notice in this data table that the manipulated variable (body mass) is the heading of one column. The responding

CALORIES BURNED IN 30 MINUTES OF ACTIVITY			
Body Mass	Experiment 1 Bicycling	Experiment 2 Playing Basketball	Experiment 3 Watching Television
30 kg	60 Calories	120 Calories	21 Calories
40 kg	77 Calories	164 Calories	27 Calories
50 kg	95 Calories	206 Calories	33 Calories
60 kg	114 Calories	248 Calories	38 Calories

variable (for Experiment 1, the number of Calories burned while bicycling) is the heading of the next column. Additional columns were added for related experiments.

Bar Graphs

To compare how many Calories a person burns doing various activities, you could create a bar graph. A bar graph is used to display data in a number of separate, or distinct, categories. In this example, bicycling, playing basketball, and watching television are three separate categories.

To create a bar graph, follow these steps.

1. On graph paper, draw a horizontal, or *x*-, axis and a vertical, or *y*-, axis.
2. Write the names of the categories to be graphed along the horizontal axis. Include an overall label for the axis as well.
3. Label the vertical axis with the name of the responding variable. Include units of measurement. Then create a scale along the axis by marking off equally spaced numbers that cover the range of the data collected.
4. For each category, draw a solid bar using the scale on the vertical axis to determine the

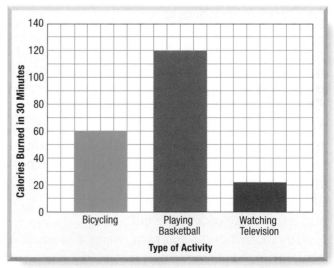

Calories Burned by a 30-kilogram Person in Various Activities

appropriate height. For example, for bicycling, draw the bar as high as the 60 mark on the vertical axis. Make all the bars the same width and leave equal spaces between them.
5. Add a title that describes the graph.

Line Graphs

To see whether a relationship exists between body mass and the number of Calories burned while bicycling, you could create a line graph. A line graph is used to display data that show how one variable (the responding variable) changes in response to another variable (the manipulated variable). You can use a line graph when your manipulated variable is *continuous*, that is, when there are other points between the ones that you tested. In this example, body mass is a continuous variable because there are other body masses between 30 and 40 kilograms (for example, 31 kilograms). Time is another example of a continuous variable.

Line graphs are powerful tools because they allow you to estimate values for conditions that you did not test in the experiment. For example, you can use the line graph to estimate that a 35-kilogram person would burn 68 Calories while bicycling.

To create a line graph, follow these steps.

1. On graph paper, draw a horizontal, or *x-*, axis and a vertical, or *y-*, axis.
2. Label the horizontal axis with the name of the manipulated variable. Label the vertical axis with the name of the responding variable. Include units of measurement.
3. Create a scale on each axis by marking off equally spaced numbers that cover the range of the data collected.
4. Plot a point on the graph for each piece of data. In the line graph above, the dotted lines show how to plot the first data point (30 kilograms and 60 Calories). Draw an imaginary vertical line extending up from the horizontal axis at the 30-kilogram mark. Then draw an imaginary horizontal line extending across from the vertical axis at the 60-Calorie mark. Plot the point where the two lines intersect.

Effect of Body Mass on Calories Burned While Bicycling

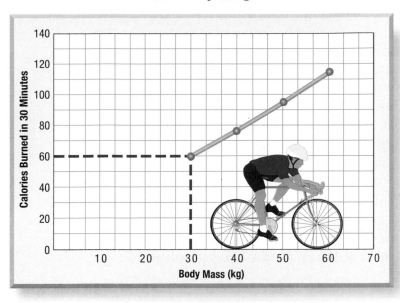

5. Connect the plotted points with a solid line. (In some cases, it may be more appropriate to draw a line that shows the general trend of the plotted points. In those cases, some of the points may fall above or below the line.)
6. Add a title that identifies the variables or relationship in the graph.

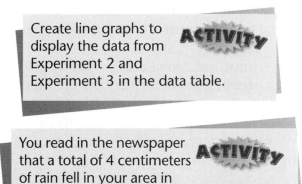

Create line graphs to display the data from Experiment 2 and Experiment 3 in the data table. **ACTIVITY**

You read in the newspaper that a total of 4 centimeters **ACTIVITY** of rain fell in your area in June, 2.5 centimeters fell in July, and 1.5 centimeters fell in August. What type of graph would you use to display these data? Use graph paper to create the graph.

Circle Graphs

Like bar graphs, circle graphs can be used to display data in a number of separate categories. Unlike bar graphs, however, circle graphs can only be used when you have data for *all* the categories that make up a given topic. A circle graph is sometimes called a pie chart because it resembles a pie cut into slices. The pie represents the entire topic, while the slices represent the individual categories. The size of a slice indicates what percentage of the whole a particular category makes up.

The data table below shows the results of a survey in which 24 teenagers were asked to identify their favorite sport. The data were then used to create the circle graph at the right.

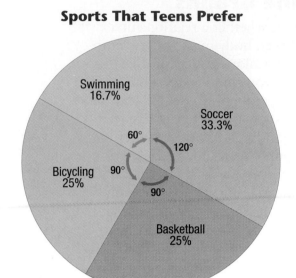

Sports That Teens Prefer

FAVORITE SPORTS	
Sport	Number of Students
Soccer	8
Basketball	6
Bicycling	6
Swimming	4

To create a circle graph, follow these steps.

1. Use a compass to draw a circle. Mark the center of the circle with a point. Then draw a line from the center point to the top of the circle.

2. Determine the size of each "slice" by setting up a proportion where x equals the number of degrees in a slice. (NOTE: A circle contains 360 degrees.) For example, to find the number of degrees in the "soccer" slice, set up the following proportion:

$$\frac{\text{students who prefer soccer}}{\text{total number of students}} = \frac{x}{\text{total number of degrees in a circle}}$$

$$\frac{8}{24} = \frac{x}{360}$$

Cross-multiply and solve for x.

$$24x = 8 \times 360$$
$$x = 120$$

The "soccer" slice should contain 120 degrees.

3. Use a protractor to measure the angle of the first slice, using the line you drew to the top of the circle as the 0° line. Draw a line from the center of the circle to the edge for the angle you measured.

4. Continue around the circle by measuring the size of each slice with the protractor. Start measuring from the edge of the previous slice so the wedges do not overlap. When you are done, the entire circle should be filled in.

5. Determine the percentage of the whole circle that each slice represents. To do this, divide the number of degrees in a slice by the total number of degrees in a circle (360), and multiply by 100%. For the "soccer" slice, you can find the percentage as follows:

$$\frac{120}{360} \times 100\% = 33.3\%$$

6. Use a different color to shade in each slice. Label each slice with the name of the category and with the percentage of the whole it represents.

7. Add a title to the circle graph.

ACTIVITY

In a class of 28 students, 12 students take the bus to school, 10 students walk, and 6 students ride their bicycles. Create a circle graph to display these data.

Laboratory Safety

Safety Symbols

These symbols alert you to possible dangers in the laboratory and remind you to work carefully.

Safety Goggles Always wear safety goggles to protect your eyes in any activity involving chemicals, flames or heating, or the possibility of broken glassware.

Lab Apron Wear a laboratory apron to protect your skin and clothing from damage.

Breakage You are working with materials that may be breakable, such as glass containers, glass tubing, thermometers, or funnels. Handle breakable materials with care. Do not touch broken glassware.

Heat-resistant Gloves Use an oven mitt or other hand protection when handling hot materials. Hot plates, hot glassware, or hot water can cause burns. Do not touch hot objects with your bare hands.

Heating Use a clamp or tongs to pick up hot glassware. Do not touch hot objects with your bare hands.

Sharp Object Pointed-tip scissors, scalpels, knives, needles, pins, or tacks are sharp. They can cut or puncture your skin. Always direct a sharp edge or point away from yourself and others. Use sharp instruments only as instructed.

Electric Shock Avoid the possibility of electric shock. Never use electrical equipment around water, or when the equipment is wet or your hands are wet. Be sure cords are untangled and cannot trip anyone. Disconnect the equipment when it is not in use.

Corrosive Chemical You are working with an acid or another corrosive chemical. Avoid getting it on your skin or clothing, or in your eyes. Do not inhale the vapors. Wash your hands when you are finished with the activity.

Poison Do not let any poisonous chemical come in contact with your skin, and do not inhale its vapors. Wash your hands when you are finished with the activity.

Physical Safety When an experiment involves physical activity, take precautions to avoid injuring yourself or others. Follow instructions from your teacher. Alert your teacher if there is any reason you should not participate in the activity.

Animal Safety Treat live animals with care to avoid harming the animals or yourself. Working with animal parts or preserved animals also may require caution. Wash your hands when you are finished with the activity.

Plant Safety Handle plants in the laboratory or during field work only as directed by your teacher. If you are allergic to certain plants, tell your teacher before doing an activity in which those plants are used. Avoid touching harmful plants such as poison ivy, poison oak, or poison sumac, or plants with thorns. Wash your hands when you are finished with the activity.

Flames You may be working with flames from a lab burner, candle, or matches. Tie back loose hair and clothing. Follow instructions from your teacher about lighting and extinguishing flames.

No Flames Flammable materials may be present. Make sure there are no flames, sparks, or other exposed heat sources present.

Fumes When poisonous or unpleasant vapors may be involved, work in a ventilated area. Avoid inhaling vapors directly. Only test an odor when directed to do so by your teacher, and use a wafting motion to direct the vapor toward your nose.

Disposal Chemicals and other laboratory materials used in the activity must be disposed of safely. Follow the instructions from your teacher.

Hand Washing Wash your hands thoroughly when finished with the activity. Use antibacterial soap and warm water. Lather both sides of your hands and between your fingers. Rinse well.

General Safety Awareness You may see this symbol when none of the symbols described earlier appears. In this case, follow the specific instructions provided. You may also see this symbol when you are asked to develop your own procedure in a lab. Have your teacher approve your plan before you go further.

Science Safety Rules

To prepare yourself to work safely in the laboratory, read over the following safety rules. Then read them a second time. Make sure you understand and follow each rule. Ask your teacher to explain any rules you do not understand.

Dress Code

1. To protect yourself from injuring your eyes, wear safety goggles whenever you work with chemicals, burners, glassware, or any substance that might get into your eyes. If you wear contact lenses, notify your teacher.
2. Wear a lab apron or coat whenever you work with corrosive chemicals or substances that can stain.
3. Tie back long hair to keep it away from any chemicals, flames, or equipment.
4. Remove or tie back any article of clothing or jewelry that can hang down and touch chemicals, flames, or equipment. Roll up or secure long sleeves.
5. Never wear open shoes or sandals.

General Precautions

6. Read all directions for an experiment several times before beginning the activity. Carefully follow all written and oral instructions. If you are in doubt about any part of the experiment, ask your teacher for assistance.
7. Never perform activities that are not assigned or authorized by your teacher. Obtain permission before "experimenting" on your own. Never handle any equipment unless you have specific permission.
8. Never perform lab activities without direct supervision.
9. Never eat or drink in the laboratory.
10. Keep work areas clean and tidy at all times. Bring only notebooks and lab manuals or written lab procedures to the work area. All other items, such as purses and backpacks, should be left in a designated area.
11. Do not engage in horseplay.

First Aid

12. Always report all accidents or injuries to your teacher, no matter how minor. Notify your teacher immediately about any fires.
13. Learn what to do in case of specific accidents, such as getting acid in your eyes or on your skin. (Rinse acids from your body with lots of water.)
14. Be aware of the location of the first-aid kit, but do not use it unless instructed by your teacher. In case of injury, your teacher should administer first aid. Your teacher may also send you to the school nurse or call a physician.
15. Know the location of emergency equipment, such as the fire extinguisher and fire blanket, and know how to use it.
16. Know the location of the nearest telephone and whom to contact in an emergency.

Heating and Fire Safety

17. Never use a heat source, such as a candle, burner, or hot plate, without wearing safety goggles.
18. Never heat anything unless instructed to do so. A chemical that is harmless when cool may be dangerous when heated.
19. Keep all combustible materials away from flames. Never use a flame or spark near a combustible chemical.
20. Never reach across a flame.
21. Before using a laboratory burner, make sure you know proper procedures for lighting and adjusting the burner, as demonstrated by your teacher. Do not touch the burner. It may be hot. And never leave a lighted burner unattended!
22. Chemicals can splash or boil out of a heated test tube. When heating a substance in a test tube, make sure that the mouth of the tube is not pointed at you or anyone else.
23. Never heat a liquid in a closed container. The expanding gases produced may blow the container apart.
24. Before picking up a container that has been heated, hold the back of your hand near it. If you can feel heat on the back of your hand, the container is too hot to handle. Use an oven mitt to pick up a container that has been heated.

Using Chemicals Safely

25. Never mix chemicals "for the fun of it." You might produce a dangerous, possibly explosive substance.

26. Never put your face near the mouth of a container that holds chemicals. Never touch, taste, or smell a chemical unless you are instructed by your teacher to do so. Many chemicals are poisonous.

27. Use only those chemicals needed in the activity. Read and double-check labels on supply bottles before removing any chemicals. Take only as much as you need. Keep all containers closed when chemicals are not being used.

28. Dispose of all chemicals as instructed by your teacher. To avoid contamination, never return chemicals to their original containers. Never simply pour chemicals or other substances into the sink or trash containers.

29. Be extra careful when working with acids or bases. Pour all chemicals over the sink or a container, not over your work surface.

30. If you are instructed to test for odors, use a wafting motion to direct the odors to your nose. Do not inhale the fumes directly from the container.

31. When mixing an acid and water, always pour the water into the container first and then add the acid to the water. Never pour water into an acid.

32. Take extreme care not to spill any material in the laboratory. Wash chemical spills and splashes immediately with plenty of water. Immediately begin rinsing with water any acids that get on your skin or clothing, and notify your teacher of any acid spill at the same time.

Using Glassware Safely

33. Never force glass tubing or thermometers into a rubber stopper or rubber tubing. Have your teacher insert the glass tubing or thermometer if required for an activity.

34. If you are using a laboratory burner, use a wire screen to protect glassware from any flame. Never heat glassware that is not thoroughly dry on the outside.

35. Keep in mind that hot glassware looks cool. Never pick up glassware without first checking to see if it is hot. Use an oven mitt. See rule 24.

36. Never use broken or chipped glassware. If glassware breaks, notify your teacher and dispose of the glassware in the proper broken-glassware container. Never handle broken glass with your bare hands.

37. Never eat or drink from lab glassware.

38. Thoroughly clean glassware before putting it away.

Using Sharp Instruments

39. Handle scalpels or other sharp instruments with extreme care. Never cut material toward you; cut away from you.

40. Immediately notify your teacher if you cut your skin when working in the laboratory.

Animal and Plant Safety

41. Never perform experiments that cause pain, discomfort, or harm to mammals, birds, reptiles, fishes, or amphibians. This rule applies at home as well as in the classroom.

42. Animals should be handled only if absolutely necessary. Your teacher will instruct you as to how to handle each animal species brought into the classroom.

43. If you know that you are allergic to certain plants, molds, or animals, tell your teacher before doing an activity in which these are used.

44. During field work, protect your skin by wearing long pants, long sleeves, socks, and closed shoes. Know how to recognize the poisonous plants and fungi in your area, as well as plants with thorns, and avoid contact with them.

45. Never eat any part of an unidentified plant or fungus.

46. Wash your hands thoroughly after handling animals or the cage containing animals. Wash your hands when you are finished with any activity involving animal parts, plants, or soil.

End-of-Experiment Rules

47. After an experiment has been completed, clean up your work area and return all equipment to its proper place.

48. Dispose of waste materials as instructed by your teacher.

49. Wash your hands after every experiment.

50. Always turn off all burners or hot plates when they are not in use. Unplug hot plates and other electrical equipment. If you used a burner, check that the gas-line valve to the burner is off as well.

Using a Laboratory Balance

The laboratory balance is an important tool in scientific investigations. You can use a balance to determine the masses of materials that you study or experiment with in the laboratory.

Different kinds of balances are used in the laboratory. One kind of balance is the triple-beam balance. The balance that you may use in your science class is probably similar to the balance illustrated in this Appendix. To use the balance properly, you should learn the name, location, and function of each part of the balance you are using. What kind of balance do you have in your science class?

The Triple-Beam Balance

The triple-beam balance is a single-pan balance with three beams calibrated in grams. The back, or 100-gram, beam is divided into ten units of 10 grams each. The middle, or 500-gram, beam is divided into five units of 100 grams each. The front, or 10-gram, beam is divided into ten major units of 1 gram each. Each of these units is further divided into units of 0.1 gram. What is the largest mass you could find with a triple-beam balance?

The following procedure can be used to find the mass of an object with a triple-beam balance:

1. Place the object on the pan.
2. Move the rider on the middle beam notch by notch until the horizontal pointer drops below zero. Move the rider back one notch.
3. Move the rider on the back beam notch by notch until the pointer again drops below zero. Move the rider back one notch.
4. Slowly slide the rider along the front beam until the pointer stops at the zero point.
5. The mass of the object is equal to the sum of the readings on the three beams.

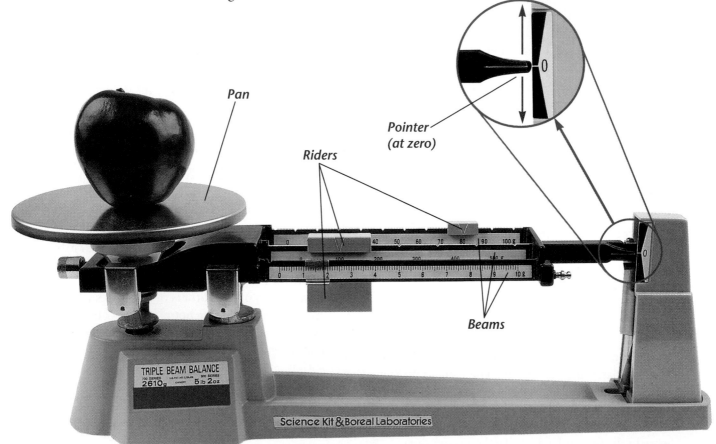

Triple-Beam Balance

List of Chemical Elements

Name	Symbol	Atomic Number	Atomic Mass†
Actinium	Ac	89	227.028
Aluminum	Al	13	26.982
Americium	Am	95	(243)
Antimony	Sb	51	121.75
Argon	Ar	18	39.948
Arsenic	As	33	74.922
Astatine	At	85	(210)
Barium	Ba	56	137.327
Berkelium	Bk	97	(247)
Beryllium	Be	4	9.012
Bismuth	Bi	83	208.980
Bohrium	Bh	107	(262)
Boron	B	5	10.811
Bromine	Br	35	79.904
Cadmium	Cd	48	112.411
Calcium	Ca	20	40.078
Californium	Cf	98	(251)
Carbon	C	6	12.011
Cerium	Ce	58	140.115
Cesium	Cs	55	132.905
Chlorine	Cl	17	35.453
Chromium	Cr	24	51.996
Cobalt	Co	27	58.933
Copper	Cu	29	63.546
Curium	Cm	96	(247)
Dubnium	Db	105	(262)
Dysprosium	Dy	66	162.50
Einsteinium	Es	99	(252)
Erbium	Er	68	167.26
Europium	Eu	63	151.965
Fermium	Fm	100	(257)
Fluorine	F	9	18.998
Francium	Fr	87	(223)
Gadolinium	Gd	64	157.25
Gallium	Ga	31	69.723
Germanium	Ge	32	72.61
Gold	Au	79	196.967
Hafnium	Hf	72	178.49
Hassium	Hs	108	(265)
Helium	He	2	4.003
Holmium	Ho	67	164.930
Hydrogen	H	1	1.008
Indium	In	49	114.818
Iodine	I	53	126.904
Iridium	Ir	77	192.22
Iron	Fe	26	55.847
Krypton	Kr	36	83.80
Lanthanum	La	57	138.906
Lawrencium	Lr	103	(260)
Lead	Pb	82	207.2
Lithium	Li	3	6.941
Lutetium	Lu	71	174.967
Magnesium	Mg	12	24.305
Manganese	Mn	25	54.938
Meitnerium	Mt	109	(266)
Mendelevium	Md	101	(258)
Mercury	Hg	80	200.659
Molybdenum	Mo	42	95.94
Neodymium	Nd	60	144.2
Neon	Ne	10	20.180
Neptunium	Np	93	237.048
Nickel	Ni	28	58.69
Niobium	Nb	41	92.906
Nitrogen	N	7	14.007
Nobelium	No	102	(259)
Osmium	Os	76	190.23
Oxygen	O	8	15.999
Palladium	Pd	46	106.42
Phosphorus	P	15	30.974
Platinum	Pt	78	195.08
Plutonium	Pu	94	(244)
Polonium	Po	84	(209)
Potassium	K	19	39.098
Praseodymium	Pr	59	140.908
Promethium	Pm	61	(145)
Protactinium	Pa	91	231.036
Radium	Ra	88	226.025
Radon	Rn	86	(222)
Rhenium	Re	75	186.207
Rhodium	Rh	45	102.906
Rubidium	Rb	37	85.468
Ruthenium	Ru	44	101.07
Rutherfordium	Rf	104	(261)
Samarium	Sm	62	150.36
Scandium	Sc	21	44.956
Seaborgium	Sg	106	(263)
Selenium	Se	34	78.96
Silicon	Si	14	28.086
Silver	Ag	47	107.868
Sodium	Na	11	22.990
Strontium	Sr	38	87.62
Sulfur	S	16	32.066
Tantalum	Ta	73	180.948
Technetium	Tc	43	(98)
Tellurium	Te	52	127.60
Terbium	Tb	65	158.925
Thallium	Tl	81	204.383
Thorium	Th	90	232.038
Thulium	Tm	69	168.934
Tin	Sn	50	118.710
Titanium	Ti	22	47.88
Tungsten	W	74	183.85
Ununnilium	Uun	110	(269)
Unununium	Uuu	111	(272)
Ununbium	Uub	112	(272)
Uranium	U	92	238.029
Vanadium	V	23	50.942
Xenon	Xe	54	131.29
Ytterbium	Yb	70	173.04
Yttrium	Y	39	88.906
Zinc	Zn	30	65.39
Zirconium	Zr	40	91.224

†Numbers in parentheses give the mass number of the most stable isotope.

Periodic Table of the Elements

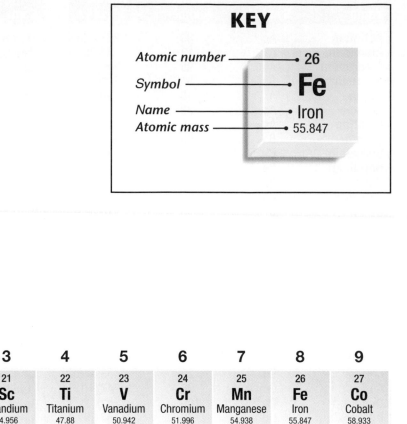

KEY

Atomic number —— 26
Symbol —— **Fe**
Name —— Iron
Atomic mass —— 55.847

1

1
H
Hydrogen
1.008

2

3	4
Li	**Be**
Lithium	Beryllium
6.941	9.012

11	12
Na	**Mg**
Sodium	Magnesium
22.990	24.305

	3	4	5	6	7	8	9
19	21	22	23	24	25	26	27
K	**Sc**	**Ti**	**V**	**Cr**	**Mn**	**Fe**	**Co**
	20						
	Ca						

Row 4:
19	20	21	22	23	24	25	26	27
K	**Ca**	**Sc**	**Ti**	**V**	**Cr**	**Mn**	**Fe**	**Co**
Potassium	Calcium	Scandium	Titanium	Vanadium	Chromium	Manganese	Iron	Cobalt
39.098	40.078	44.956	47.88	50.942	51.996	54.938	55.847	58.933

37	38	39	40	41	42	43	44	45
Rb	**Sr**	**Y**	**Zr**	**Nb**	**Mo**	**Tc**	**Ru**	**Rh**
Rubidium	Strontium	Yttrium	Zirconium	Niobium	Molybdenum	Technetium	Ruthenium	Rhodium
85.468	87.62	88.906	91.224	92.906	95.94	(98)	101.07	102.906

55	56	57	72	73	74	75	76	77
Cs	**Ba**	**La**	**Hf**	**Ta**	**W**	**Re**	**Os**	**Ir**
Cesium	Barium	Lanthanum	Hafnium	Tantalum	Tungsten	Rhenium	Osmium	Iridium
132.905	137.327	138.906	178.49	180.948	183.85	186.207	190.23	192.22

87	88	89	104	105	106	107	108	109
Fr	**Ra**	**Ac**	**Rf**	**Db**	**Sg**	**Bh**	**Hs**	**Mt**
Francium	Radium	Actinium	Rutherfordium	Dubnium	Seaborgium	Bohrium	Hassium	Meitnerium
(223)	226.025	227.028	(261)	(262)	(263)	(262)	(265)	(266)

Lanthanide Series

58	59	60	61	62
Ce	**Pr**	**Nd**	**Pm**	**Sm**
Cerium	Praseodymium	Neodymium	Promethium	Samarium
140.115	140.908	144.24	(145)	150.36

Actinide Series

90	91	92	93	94
Th	**Pa**	**U**	**Np**	**Pu**
Thorium	Protactinium	Uranium	Neptunium	Plutonium
232.038	231.036	238.029	237.048	(244)

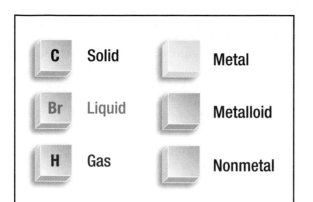

			18
			2 **He** Helium 4.003

13	14	15	16	17	
5 **B** Boron 10.811	6 **C** Carbon 12.011	7 **N** Nitrogen 14.007	8 **O** Oxygen 15.999	9 **F** Fluorine 18.998	10 **Ne** Neon 20.180
13 **Al** Aluminum 26.982	14 **Si** Silicon 28.086	15 **P** Phosphorus 30.974	16 **S** Sulfur 32.066	17 **Cl** Chlorine 35.453	18 **Ar** Argon 39.948

10	11	12						
28 **Ni** Nickel 58.69	29 **Cu** Copper 63.546	30 **Zn** Zinc 65.39	31 **Ga** Gallium 69.723	32 **Ge** Germanium 72.61	33 **As** Arsenic 74.922	34 **Se** Selenium 78.96	35 **Br** Bromine 79.904	36 **Kr** Krypton 83.80
46 **Pd** Palladium 106.42	47 **Ag** Silver 107.868	48 **Cd** Cadmium 112.411	49 **In** Indium 114.818	50 **Sn** Tin 118.710	51 **Sb** Antimony 121.75	52 **Te** Tellurium 127.60	53 **I** Iodine 126.904	54 **Xe** Xenon 131.29
78 **Pt** Platinum 195.08	79 **Au** Gold 196.967	80 **Hg** Mercury 200.59	81 **Tl** Thallium 204.383	82 **Pb** Lead 207.2	83 **Bi** Bismuth 208.980	84 **Po** Polonium (209)	85 **At** Astatine (210)	86 **Rn** Radon (222)
110 **Uun** Ununnilium (269)	111 **Uuu** Unununium (272)	112 **Uub** Ununbium (272)						

The symbols shown for elements 110-112 are being used temporarily until names for these elements can be agreed upon.

63 **Eu** Europium 151.965	64 **Gd** Gadolinium 157.25	65 **Tb** Terbium 158.925	66 **Dy** Dysprosium 162.50	67 **Ho** Holmium 164.930	68 **Er** Erbium 167.26	69 **Tm** Thulium 168.934	70 **Yb** Ytterbium 173.04	71 **Lu** Lutetium 174.967
95 **Am** Americium (243)	96 **Cm** Curium (247)	97 **Bk** Berkelium (247)	98 **Cf** Californium (251)	99 **Es** Einsteinium (252)	100 **Fm** Fermium (257)	101 **Md** Mendelevium (258)	102 **No** Nobelium (259)	103 **Lr** Lawrencium (260)

Mass numbers in parentheses are those of the most stable or common isotope.

Glossary

acid A substance that tastes sour, reacts with metals and carbonates, and turns blue litmus red. (p. 90)

activation energy The minimum amount of energy that has to be added to get a chemical reaction started. (p. 33)

alloy A substance made of two or more elements that has the properties of metal. (p. 123)

alpha particle A type of nuclear radiation consisting of two protons and two neutrons. (p. 135)

atom The smallest particle of an element. (p. 20)

atomic number The number of protons in the nucleus of an atom. (p. 55)

B

base A substance that tastes bitter, feels slippery, and turns red litmus blue. (p. 95)

beta particle An electron that is given off as nuclear radiation. (p. 135)

C

catalyst A material that increases the rate of a chemical reaction by lowering the activation energy. (p. 36)

cellulose A flexible but strong natural polymer that gives shape to plant cells. (p. 114)

ceramic A hard, crystalline solid made by heating clay and other mineral materials to high temperatures. (p. 128)

chemical bond The force that holds atoms together. (p. 21)

chemical change A change in matter that produces a new substance. (p. 17)

chemical digestion The process that breaks large food molecules into smaller molecules. (p. 104)

chemical equation A short, easy way to show chemical reactions, using symbols instead of words. (p. 24)

chemical formula A combination of symbols that represent the elements in a compound. (p. 25)

chemical reaction The process in which substances undergo chemical changes that results in the formation of new substances. (p. 17)

chemistry The study of the properties of matter and how matter changes. (p. 14)

coefficient A number in front of a chemical formula in an equation that indicates how many molecules or atoms of each reactant and product are involved in a reaction. (p. 28)

combustion A rapid reaction between oxygen and fuel that results in fire. (p. 40)

composite A combination of two or more substances that creates a new material. (p. 116)

compound A substance made of two or more elements chemically combined in a specific ratio, or proportion. (p. 16)

concentrated solution A mixture that has a lot of solute dissolved in it. (p. 83)

concentration The amount of one material in a certain volume of another material. (p. 35)

conservation of mass The principle stating that matter is not created or destroyed during a chemical reaction. (p. 27)

controlled experiment An experiment in which all factors except one are kept constant. (p. 155)

corrosive The way in which acids react with some metals so as to eat away the metal. (p. 91)

covalent bond A chemical bond formed when two atoms share electrons. (p. 65)

crystal An orderly, three-dimensional pattern of ions or atoms in a solid. (p. 63)

D

decomposition A chemical reaction that breaks down compounds into simpler products. (p. 30)

digestion The process that breaks down complex molecules of food into smaller molecules. (p. 104)

dilute solution A mixture that has little solute dissolved in it. (p. 83)

double bond A chemical bond formed when atoms share two pairs of electrons. (p. 66)

E

electron dot diagram A representation of the number of valence electrons in an atom, using dots placed around the symbol of an element. (p. 54)

electrons Tiny, negatively charged, high-energy particles that move around outside the nucleus of an atom. (p. 51)

element A substance that cannot be broken down into any other substances by chemical or physical means. (p. 15)

endothermic reaction A reaction that absorbs energy in the form of heat. (p. 33)

enzyme A biological catalyst that lowers the activation energy of reactions in cells. (p. 37)

exothermic reaction A reaction that releases energy in the form of heat. (p. 33)

family Elements in the same vertical column of the periodic table. Also called group. (p. 56)

fuel A material that releases energy when it burns. (p. 40)

gamma radiation A type of nuclear radiation made of high-energy waves. (p. 135)

glass A clear, solid material with no crystal structure, created by heating sand to a very high temperature. (p. 130)

group Elements in the same vertical column of the periodic table. Also called family. (p. 56)

half-life The length of time needed for half the mass of a radioactive isotope to decay. (p. 136)

halogen An element belonging to Group 17 of the periodic table. (p. 57)

hydrogen ion A positively charged ion (H^+) formed of a hydrogen atom that has lost its electron. (p. 96)

hydroxide ion A negatively charged ion made of oxygen and hydrogen, OH^-. (p. 97)

hypothesis A prediction about the outcome of an experiment. (p. 154)

indicator A compound that changes color in the presence of an acid or a base. (p. 92)

inhibitor A material that decreases the rate of a reaction. (p. 37)

ion An atom or group of atoms that has become electrically charged. (p. 60)

ionic bond The attraction between oppositely charged ions. (p. 60)

isotope An atom with the same number of protons and different number of neutrons from other atoms of the same element. (p. 134)

manipulated variable The one factor that a scientist changes during an experiment. (p. 155)

mass number The sum of the protons and neutrons in the nucleus of an atom. (p. 134)

mechanical digestion The physical process that tears, grinds, and mashes large food particles into smaller ones. (p. 104)

mineral A naturally occurring solid that has a crystal structure and a definite chemical composition. (p. 72)

mixture Two or more substances that are mixed together but not chemically combined. (p. 16)

molecular compound A compound consisting of molecules of covalently bonded atoms. (p. 66)

molecule The combination of two or more atoms. (p. 20)

monomer Small, carbon-based molecules from which polymers are built. (p. 113)

neutralization A reaction of an acid with a base, yielding a solution that is not as acidic or basic as the starting solutions were. (p. 100)

neutrons Small uncharged particles that are found in the nucleus of an atom. (p. 51)

nonpolar The description of a covalent bond in which electrons are shared equally, or of a molecule containing nonpolar bonds, or polar bonds that cancel out. (p. 68)

nuclear radiation Particles and energy released from a radioactive nucleus. (p. 135)

nuclear reaction A reaction involving the particles in the nucleus of an atom that can change one element into another element. (p. 134)

nucleus The central core of the atom, containing protons and usually neutrons. (p. 51)

operational definition A statement that describes how a particular variable is to be measured or a term is to be defined. (p. 155)

optical fiber A threadlike piece of glass that can be used for transmitting messages in the form of light. (p. 131)

period Elements in the same horizontal row of the periodic table. (p. 56)

pH scale A measure of the concentration of hydrogen ions in a solution. (p. 98)

physical change A change that alters the form or appearance of a material but does not make the material into another substance. (p. 17)

plastic A synthetic polymer that can be molded or shaped. (p. 115)

polar The description of a covalent bond in which electrons are shared unequally, or of a molecule containing polar bonds that do not cancel out. (p. 67)

polyatomic ion An ion that is made of more than one atom. (p. 62)

polymer A large, complex, carbon-based molecule built from smaller molecules joined together. (p. 113)

precipitate A solid that forms from a solution during a chemical reaction. (p. 18)

product A substance formed as a result of a chemical reaction. (p. 26)

protons Small positively charged particles that are found in the nucleus of an atom. (p. 51)

radiation therapy A process in which radioactive elements are used to destroy unhealthy cells. (p. 138)

radioactive dating The process of determining the age of an object using the half-life of one or more radioactive isotopes. (p. 136)

radioactive decay The process in which the atomic nuclei of unstable isotopes release fast-moving particles and energy. (p. 134)

reactant A substance that enters into a chemical reaction. (p. 26)

replacement reaction A reaction in which one element replaces another in a compound; or when two elements in different compounds trade places. (p. 31)

responding variable The factor that changes as a result of changes to the manipulated variable in an experiment. (p. 155)

salt An ionic compound that can form from the neutralization of an acid with a base. (p. 101)

saturated solution A mixture that has so much solute in it that no more will dissolve. (p. 84)

solubility A measure of how well a solute can dissolve in a solvent at a given temperature. (p. 84)

solute The part of a solution present in a lesser amount and that is dissolved by the solvent. (p. 81)

solution A well-mixed mixture. (p. 16)

solvent The part of a solution present in the largest amount and that dissolves other substances. (p. 81)

subscript A number in a chemical formula that tells the number of atoms in a molecule or the ratio of elements in a compound. (p. 25)

suspension A mixture in which particles can be seen and easily separated by settling or filtration. (p. 80)

symbol A one- or two-letter set of characters that is used to identify elements. (p. 25)

synthesis A chemical reaction in which two or more simple substances combine to form a new, more complex substance. (p. 29)

········ T ········

tracer A radioactive isotope that can be followed through the steps of a chemical reaction or industrial process. (p. 137)

········ U ········

unsaturated solution A mixture in which more solute can be dissolved. (p. 84)

········ V ········

valence electrons The electrons that are farthest away from the nucleus of an atom and are involved in chemical reactions. (p. 53)

variable Any factor that can change in an experiment. (p. 155)

Index

—54, 56–57 59–61, 65, 66
dot diagrams 54, 65, 66, 68
electron sharing 65–66
  unequal 67–68
electron transfer 59–61
element 15
  comparing families of 56–57
  defined 15
  list of 167
  organizing 55–56
  periodic table of 55–58, 168–169
  radioactive 133–140
  symbols for 25
endothermic reaction 33
energy
  activation 33–34
  in chemical reactions 33
enzymes 37, 38–39
  digestive 105, 106
equations, chemical. *See* chemical equations.
etching 91
evidence, for chemical reactions 18, 19, 22–23
exothermic reaction 33
experiments. *See* scientific investigations.

families, in periodic table 56–57
fiberglass 117, 118
fire(s) 40–43
  baking soda and 40, 42–43
  controlling 41–42
  fighting 42–43
  necessary ingredients of 41
  prevention of 43
  sources of 42
fire extinguishers 43
fire-safe house 43
fire safety 42–43
fire triangle 41
flowcharts 159
fluorine 65, 68
forming operational definitions 155
formulas. *See* chemical formulas.
fossils 136, 137
freezing points, of solutions 86
fuel 40

gamma decay 135
gamma radiation 135, 137–138
gamma rays 135, 137–138
gas production 19
generalizations, skill of making 157
glass 130–131
  in optical fibers 131–132
gluten 147
gold, in aircraft 125
gold alloys 124
Goodyear, Charles 116
graphs 160–162
grocery bags 122
groups, in periodic table 56–57

half-life 136, 137, 140
halite, bonding in 73–74

halite crystal 63
halogen family 57
hazardous chemicals, transporting 44
Hazardous Materials Transportation Act 44
heat
  for fire 41
  and rate of chemical reaction 36
high-density polyethylene (HDPE) 115
Hindenburg 34
home fire safety 42–43
hydrogen ions, in solution 97, 98–99
hydroxide ion 97, 98
hypothesis 154

illustrations, skill of interpreting 156
indicators 79, 92, 95, 99
inert (noble) gases 57
inferring, skill of 150
inhibitors, of chemical reactions 37
interpreting data, skill of 155
interpreting illustrations, skill of 156
ion(s) 60
  polyatomic 62
  positive and negative 60–64
ionic bonds 59–64
  defined 60
  exploring 61
  forming 60
ionic compounds
  crystal shape of 63
  electrical conductivity of 64
  formation of 60–61
  melting points of 64
  naming 62
  properties of 63–64
ionic crystal 63, 73–74
ionic solids, in water 82
ion implantation 124
iron alloys 126
  in aircraft 125
isotopes 134
  using 136–138

judgments, skill of making 157

Kevlar 117
Knickerbocker, Janet 148–149

laboratory balance 166
laboratory safety 163–165
leavening agent 144, 146
length, measuring 152
light-emitting polymers (LEPs) 117
lignin 117
litmus paper 90, 92, 95
low-density polyethylene (LDPE) 115

making generalizations, skill of 157
making judgments, skill of 157
making models, skill of 151
manipulated variable 155
mass
  conservation of 26–27
  measuring 153

mass number 134
matter
  building blocks of 15–16
  changes in 17–18
  conservation of 27
measuring, skill of 152–153
mechanical digestion 104
melting points
  of ionic compounds 64
  of molecular compounds 66–67
metal(s)
  in aircraft 125
  properties of 123
  reactions of acids with 91
  reactive 57
  Wood's 126
metal etching 91
mica 73
mineral(s)
  defined 72
  properties of 72–73
mineral crystals, bonding in 73–74
mixtures 16
models
  of atoms 52–53
  skill of making 151
molecular compounds 66–67
molecular solids, in water 83
molecules 20–21
  attractions between 68–69
  nonpolar 68
  polar 68–69
Molina, Mario 8–11
monomers 113
mouth, pH of 105

Nagaoka, Hantara 52
natural composites 117
natural polymers 114
negative ions 60, 62, 63
neutralization 100, 101
neutral solution 100
neutrons 51, 53, 134
nickel alloys, in aircraft 125
nitroglycerin 37
Nobel, Alfred 37
noble (inert) gases 57
nonmetals, reactive 57
nonpolar bond 68
nonpolar molecules 68, 69
nonpolar solvents 85
nuclear power 138
nuclear reactions 134
nucleus 51, 134
nylon 115, 117

observing, skill of 150
operational definitions 155
optical fibers 131–132
oxygen 66
  for fire 41
  in covalent bonds 66, 68–69
ozone 9
ozone hole 10, 11
ozone layer 8–11

Index

...edgments

...rds & Associates: 52bl, 99
...a Golden: 6, 62b, 144, 147
...ared Lee: 34, 60, 87
Martucci Design: 47, 54, 57, 61, 65, 66, 68, 143, 160, 161, 162,
Matt Mayerchak: 46, 76, 105t, 108, 113, 158, 159,
Fran Milner: 105br
Morgan Cain & Associates: 7, 9, 21, 24, 28, 33, 36, 37, 41, 43, 51, 52t, 52br,
53, 56, 63, 69t, 73, 82, 86, 98, 109, 134, 152, 153, 156, 168–169
Scott Sawyer: 148, 149
Nancy Smith: 22, 38, 58, 70, 88, 102, 120, 140
J/B Woolsey Associates: 135, 137

Photography

Photo Research by Sue McDermott
Cover image Brian Sytnyk/Masterfile

Nature of Science
Page 8t, Joe Towers/The Stock Market; **8b,** Bourg/Liaison International; **9,** Leonard Lessin/Peter Arnold; **10–11 both,** NASA.

Chapter 1
Pages 12–13, Kunio Owaki/The Stock Market; **14,** Mark Wagner/TSI; **15l,** Cathlyn Melloan/TSI; **15m,** Bernard Roussel/The Image Bank; **15r,** Bob Firth/International Stock; **16,** Russ Lappa; **17,** Bob Firth/International Stock; **18,** Steve Elmore/The Stock Market; **19t,** Charles D. Winters/Photo Researchers; **19bl,** Russ Lappa; **19ml,** Wood Sabold/International Stock; **19mr,** Ken O'Donaghue; **19br,** Steven Needham/ Envision; **20l,** Russ Lappa; **20r,** J. Sulley/The Image Works; **21,** Ken Eward/Science Source/Photo Researchers; **23,** Richard Haynes; **24, 26 all,** Russ Lappa; **27,** John D. Cummingham/Visuals Unlimited; **29,** Koitsu Hirota/The Image Bank; **30,** Paul Sisul/TSI; **31t,** Russ Lappa; **31b,** Charles D. Winters/Photo Researchers; **32t,** Richard Haynes; **32b,** Simon Norfolk/TSI; **33,** Michael Newman/PhotoEdit; **35tl & tr,** Richard Megna/Fundamental Photographs; **35b,** AP/Wide World Photos; **36, 38,** Russ Lappa; **39, 40t,** Richard Haynes; **40b,** Patrick Donehue/Photo Researchers; **41,** Dorothy Littell/Stock Boston; **42 all,** Russ Lappa; **44,** Dede Gilman/Photo Network; **45l,** Steven Needham/Envision; **45r,** Richard Megna/Fundamental Photographs.

Chapter 2
Pages 48–49, Ken Eward/Science Source/Photo Researchers; **50, 51 both, 52tl,tr, 53t,** Russ Lappa; **53b,** Frank Cezus/FPG International; **55,** Richard Megna/ Fundamental Photographs; **59t,** Russ Lappa; **59b,** Arthur Gurmankin & Mary Morina/ Visuals Unlimited; **61tl,** Lawrence Migdale/Photo Researchers; **61tr,** Richard Megna/ Fundamental Photographs; **61b, 62,** Russ Lappa; **63,** M. Claye/Jacana/Photo Researchers; **64,** Richard Megna/ Fundamental Photograhs; **65,** Russ Lappa; **67,** George Disario/The Stock Market; **70, 71,** Richard Haynes; **72l,** Gary Retherford/ Photo Researchers; **72r, 73l, m,** Paul Silverman/Fundamental Photographs; **73r,** Ken Lucas/Visuals Unlimited; **74t,** Breck P. Kent/Earth Scenes; **74b,** Russ Lappa; **75,** George Disario/The Stock Market.

Chapter 3
Pages 78–79, Minolta Corp.; **80,** Michael Newman/PhotoEdit; **81t, m,** Russ Lappa; **81b,** Leonard Lessin/Peter Arnold; **83,** Russ Lappa; **84,** Tony Freeman/PhotoEdit; **85, 88,** Russ Lappa; **89,** Richard Haynes; **90t,** Russ Lappa; **90b,** Lawrence Migdale/ Photo Researchers; **91 both,** Russ Lappa; **92,** Bob Krist/The Stock Market; **93tl,** Russ Lappa; **93tr,** David Young-Wolfe/PhotoEdit; **93bl,** Mark C. Burnett/Stock Boston; **93m, br,** Russ Lappa; **94br,** B. Daemmrich/The Image Works; **94 all others,** Russ Lappa; **95,** P. Aprahamian/ Science Photo Library/Photo Researchers; **96,** Russ Lappa; **97t,** L.S. Stepanowicz/Visuals Unlimited; **97b,** Tom Pantages; **99,** Richard Haynes; **100t,** Jenny Hager/The Image Works; **100b,** Russ Lappa; **101,** George Ranalli/Photo Researchers; **102,** Russ Lappa; **103,** Richard Haynes; **104,** Cleo Photography/Photo Researchers; **106,** Russ Lappa; **107t,** P. Aprahamian/ Science Photo Library/Photo Researchers; **107b,** Lawrence Migdale/Photo Researchers.

Chapter 4
Pages 110–111, Larry Ulrich/DRK Photo; **112,** John Terence Turner/FPG International; **113,** Russ Lappa; **114l,** Tom Tracey/The Stock Market; **114r,** Inga Spence/Visuals Unlimted; **114b,** William Whitehurst/The Stock Market; **116t,** Leonard Lessin/Peter Arnold; **116l,** Corbis-Bettmann; **116r,** Terry Wild Studio/Uniphoto; **117l,** David Young-Wolfe/PhotoEdit; **117r,** Nick Colaneri/Uniax Corporation; **117b,** Jeffry W. Myers/The Stock Market; **118l,** Bob Torrez/TSI; **118r,** David J. Sams/TSI; **119l,** Dennis O'Clair/ TSI; **119r,** Richard Hutchings/Photo Researchers; **120,** Daemmrich/Uniphoto; **121,** Richard Haynes; **122,** Tom Smith/Photo Researchers; **123t,** Russ Lappa; **123b,** Bachmann/PhotoEdit; **124l,** Richard Haynes; **124r,** Diana Calder/The Stock Market; **125t,** AP Photo/Boeing handout/Wide World; **125m,** Peter Gridley/FPG International; **125bl,** De Malglaive E./Liaison International; **125br,** Pratt & Whitney/Liaison International; **127l,** William Hopkins; **127r,** Marc Pokempner/TSI; **128t,** Russ Lappa; **128b,** M. Borchi White Star/Photo Researchers; **129t,** Daniel Aubry/The Stock Market; **129bl,** Mark Richards/PhotoEdit; **129br,** Dan McCoy/Rainbow; **130 both,** James L. Amos/Peter Arnold; **131,** D. Young-Wolff MR/PhotoEdit; **132,** Ted Horowitz/The Stock Market; **133,** Jan Van Der Straet/Granger Collection, NY; **136,** T.A. Wiewandt/DRK Photo; **138l,** Jean-Perrin/CNRI/Science Photo Library/Photo Researchers; **138r,** Alfred Pasieka/Science Photo Library/Photo Researchers; **139 both,** Pat Cunningham/Liaison International; **141t,** Inga Spence/Visuals Unlimted; **141b,** Russ Lappa.

Interdisciplinary Exploration
Page 144t, Peter Johansky/Envision; **144b,** Scott J. Witte/Index Stock Imagery; **145t,** Russ Lappa; **145m,** Bill Aron/TSI; **145b,** Steven Needham/Envision; **146t,** Tony Freeman/Photo Edit; **146–147,** Paul Chesley/TSI; **147,** Russ Lappa

Skills Handbook
Page 150, Mike Moreland/Photo Network; **151t,** Foodpix; **151m,** Richard Haynes; **151b,** Russ Lappa; **154,** Richard Haynes; **156,** Ron Kimball; **157,** Renee Lynn/Photo Researchers.